FUN
OLD TESTAMENT
BIBLE STUDIES

by Mike Gillespie

Group Books

Loveland, Colorado

Fun Old Testament Bible Studies

Copyright © 1989 by Mike Gillespie

Credits
Edited by Michael D. Warden
Book and cover design by Judy Atwood Bienick
Cover illustration by Rand Kruback

Scripture quotations are from the Holy Bible, New International Version. Copyright © 1973, 1978, 1984 International Bible Society. Used by permission of Zondervan Bible Publishers.

Library of Congress Cataloging-in-Publication Data
Gillespie, Mike, 1947-
    Fun Old Testament Bible Studies / by Mike Gillespie
      p.   cm.
    Summary: Bible studies and activities aimed at applying the Old Testament stories to modern life.
    ISBN 0-931529-64-6 :
    1. Bible stories, English—O.T. 2. Teenagers—Religious life.
[1. Conduct of life. 2. Bible stories—O.T.] I. Title.
BS551.2.G53   1989
221.6'1—dc20   89-39293
                                    CIP
                                     AC

14 13 12 11 10 9 8 7   04 03 02 01 00 99 98 97
Printed in the United States of America.

Dedication

To my precious daughters Rebecca and Sarah. They have gifted me with an understanding of what it means to be a child of God.

Acknowledgments

No resource of this magnitude is ever a solo effort. I am so thankful for the vision of Group Books to begin this project. Yet, I also humbly realize that God's Holy Spirit is the original inspirer of these studies.

A basket full of warm fuzzies for editor Cindy Hansen is not enough. It was her keen mind and intuition that strengthened the first draft of this manuscript. The editing gifts of Nancy Shaw and Michael Warden also played an important role in refining the book.

And who could ever say enough about the contributions of the art department at Group? Thank you.

I salute the youth group of First Presbyterian Church of Brandon, Florida, and St. Andrew Presbyterian in Denton, Texas, who shared spiritual insights with me that will forever shape my understanding of scripture. Their wisdom and questions provided the foundation for my exploration of the Old Testament.

Many thanks to the members of two teacher-training classes I taught in the Bethel Bible Study program at Hyde Park Presbyterian of Tampa and First Presbyterian of Brandon, Florida. These special adults increased my appetite for the Word and heightened my appreciation of Old Testament history.

To my friend, Rev. Paul Reiter, I simply say thanks for being who you are. The seeds you've planted in me bear much fruit in the pages of this resource.

Contents

Introduction

Whenever we open the pages of God's story we open our lives to the possibility of learning about God and his ways. But our intellects don't bring us close to God. Rather, we come close to God when the Holy Spirit plants within us God's powerful grace. And from that grace we gain understanding.

In the Old Testament, we meet ourselves. We meet the joy and sadness, victory and defeat so common to our lives. We discover meaning for today and find hope and promise for tomorrow. And we affirm the legacy of faith handed down through many generations.

■ Bringing the "Then" to "Now"

How do we help kids digest the wealth of knowledge in the Old Testament? How do we get them to connect the "long ago" with the "here and now"? How can we make the Old Testament relevant to kids' lives? *Fun Old Testament Bible Studies* uses five principles that can help bridge the Old Testament "gap."

● **Principle 1: Present God's Word.** Kids need to wrestle directly with scripture. Each session in this book lets the kids dig into a specific passage and discover its meaning. Kids hunger for Bible knowledge, but turn away when the "food" is tasteless and stale. The sessions in this book don't water down the scripture. Rather, each session's goal is to let the Holy Spirit use the scripture to deepen kids' understanding of God's ways.

● **Principle 2: Help kids relate God's Word to their lives.** Teenagers need to see a correlation between the drama of the Old Testament and their lives. To bridge this gap, the sessions each present an Experience to help teenagers apply the Bible to their lives. For example, kids will gain insight into worship by designing and leading a worship celebration.

● **Principle 3: Let the Holy Spirit work.** It's God's Holy Spirit that empowers young people and brings them into "aha!" times of discovery. By creating an atmosphere where God can work, we enable kids to learn more than we could ever teach them on our own.

In each session, the Grow section allows kids to think through what they've learned. This critical debriefing time opens the door for the Holy Spirit to lead kids toward new discoveries about God and themselves.

● **Principle 4: Teach kids the "big picture," not just partial snapshots.** This book highlights the entire Old Testament. Why? Because only after you wrestle with all the pieces can you understand how the puzzle fits together. Kids want to know how the whole Bible fits together. They need to see the connection between Abraham and Moses, Jacob and King David.

These sessions give an overview of Old Testament history in terms kids can understand. The sessions center on themes common to the Old Testament—themes that kids can relate to, such as forgiveness, peer pressure and friendship.

● **Principle 5: Use a variety of learning experiences.** Growing minds need variety. Using the same teaching approach week after week dulls your kids' senses and interest. The Bible provides endless potential learning experiences you can take advantage of. In this book, each session's approach differs slightly from the rest. In one session, kids learn about Old Testament events by holding a time-line relay race. In another, kids discover sin's harmful effects by acting out a judgment passage from Isaiah. A balanced variety of learning experiences maintains kids' interest and leaves them wanting more.

■ How to Prepare for These Studies

No resource can do everything to create effective Bible studies. Your leadership and willingness to do personal Bible study will play a critical role in determining your Bible studies' success. Use these tips to help you get the most from *Fun Old Testament Bible Studies*:

● **Study the Old Testament.** Familiarize yourself with the passages and material for each session. Be consistent in studying. It'll benefit you and your young people.

● **Use Bible reference books.** The following would be helpful:
(1) a commentary, such as *The Interpreter's Bible*;
(2) a Bible dictionary;
(3) a Bible atlas; and
(4) a Bible handbook.

● **Pray for the Holy Spirit to work in your kids.** Pray boldly. Ask God to give young people a desire for the Word that won't stop. Pray for God to use you in ways you've never known before. Plan each session with the prayerful understanding that *you* don't change people—*God* does.

● **Challenge your students to learn and grow with you.** Have them help prepare and lead the sessions. Kids' involvement in leadership will enhance their growth and commitment.

● **Adapt the sessions to fit your youth group's needs.** Don't limit these studies to youth meetings. They make excellent resources for fellowship programs, Sunday school, retreats, workshops, campouts and lock-ins.

● **Make your learning environment exciting.** Create an Old Testament environment in your meeting area. Wear a costume that corresponds with the session. Have Middle-Eastern foods for snacks. Create a desert environment with cactus and a tent. Play Middle-Eastern music as a background.

■ What This Resource Is All About

Fun Old Testament Bible Studies makes the Old Testament come *alive* for teenagers. The sessions teach and confront kids where they are. They explore and examine kids' beliefs and lifestyles. These sessions will enable your teenagers to grow in their knowledge of God's grace and love for them.

May God richly bless your ministry. And may his Spirit pour into your young people's lives.

Why Study the Old Testament?

■ Theme: Understanding God's purpose

This session acquaints young people with the Old Testament. It introduces young people to the drama of God's people—from the birth of a nation to the struggles of faith and disobedience. This session encourages kids to learn more about the Old Testament and how it relates to their lives.

■ Objectives

During this session participants will:
- clarify their attitudes and ideas about the Old Testament;
- memorize the basic time line of the Old Testament;
- discuss the Old Testament's relevance to their lives; and
- commit to learn more about the Old Testament.

■ Preparation

Gather newsprint, markers and masking tape. Bring a medium-size wall mirror (about 12 × 18 inches). Make a copy of the "Action Covenant" for each person. Also make two copies of the "Old Testament Progression" handout and cut them into sections as marked.

Hang four sheets of newsprint on the wall. Write one of the following statements on each sheet:
- The Old Testament is . . .
- Something I've always wondered about the Old Testament is . . .
- A story I remember from the Old Testament is . . .
- One thing I can learn from the Old Testament is . . .

The Session

■ Dig

Give kids each a marker. Ask them each to write on each sheet of newsprint their completion of the statement there. After kids write their completions, discuss what they wrote. Ask kids why they responded the way they did. For instance, if a few young people wrote they think the Old Testament is boring, ask them why they feel that way. "Why" questions, asked in a non-confrontive way, help get beyond superficial answers.

■ Discover

Say: **We've seen some of our attitudes about the Old Testament. This study will help you see the Old Testament in a new, exciting way.**

Ask:

● **Why is the Old Testament included in the Bible?**
● **What can you learn about God from the Old Testament?**
● **What part of the Old Testament interests you most? Why?**
● **How can learning about the Old Testament help you?**

■ Experience

Say: **On a scale of 1 to 10, how much do you know about the sequence of events in the Old Testament—10 being "I know it really well"?**

Discuss responses.

Then say: **Let's play a fast-paced game to find out just how quickly you can organize Old Testament history.**

Divide the group into two teams. Have each team form a circle. Give each team a set of 13 symbols and key words from the "Old Testament Progression" handout. Ask each team to select a runner. The runner will arrange the key words for the team. The runner can make suggestions, but must do what the majority of the team says.

Offer an incentive, such as "The team that solves the puzzle first will be first in line for the banana splits we'll make after the meeting."

Have each team lay its key words on the floor in the middle of the circle. Stand between the two teams so you can see both sets of key words. Say: **Each of the key words represents a major event or period in the Old Testament. They belong in a specific order according to when they occurred. For instance key word "Creation" is the first event in the Old Testament.**

On "go," tell your designated runner how to place the key words in order. When your team believes all the words are in

the right order, send your runner to me, and I'll tell you how many words are out of place. For instance, if your group has three key words in the wrong place, I'll yell "Three!" Then instruct your runner to rearrange the key words until you think you've corrected the errors. Your runner will then run to me again and I'll tell you how many errors still remain. The first team to get all the key words in the right order wins.

Start the game and continue until one of the teams has placed the words in correct order.

■ Grow

After congratulating the winning team, take its key words and tape them in the correct sequence on the wall. Then use the "Old Testament Story" on page 15 and the "Old Testament Progression" on page 16 to guide your kids to memorize the 13 major periods of the Old Testament.

After the story, practice in sequence the key words and hand motions a few times with the kids. If you like, split them back into two teams and race to see which team can go through the sequence the fastest with the most accuracy. Have fun!

■ Covenant

Give each person a pencil and an "Action Covenant." Explain that the "Action Covenant" gives kids each a chance to act on what they've learned. Have someone read aloud Genesis 17:1-8 (God's covenant with Abraham) to give an example of covenant-making in scripture.

Say: **A covenant is a binding agreement. It holds deeper meaning than a simple contract because it involves committing yourself, not just money or time. In the Old Testament, a person who broke a covenant could be sentenced to death.**

The covenants you establish during our studies involve not only an agreement with God, but also with each other. The covenants help you to put your faith into action.

Tell kids they have the freedom not to join in the covenant. Explain they shouldn't make a covenant just because others do—they need to make the decision for themselves.

Have kids who want to complete their covenants pair up and agree to encourage their partners to keep the covenant during the coming month. Ask kids each to tape their covenant on a mirror at home as a reminder.

■ Go

Gather everyone in a circle. Say: **I'll pass this mirror around the circle. As it gets to you, look at your image and complete this statement: "Without a mirror, I . . ."** For example, one person might say, "Without a mirror, I couldn't see myself clearly."

After each group member responds, say: **The Old Testament is similar to a mirror. Without it, we wouldn't understand a lot about ourselves and God. The Old Testament reveals our true character. We need to look into it to understand who we are and what God wants us to become.**

Close with prayer. Ask God to bless each young person to reflect more of Jesus.

Old Testament Story

Instruct the kids to stand where they can see you. It may help if you stand on a chair or platform. Once everyone is in place, say: **The great stories of men and women were passed down through the generations by word of mouth. I'm going to tell one of the greatest stories that can be told. As I tell it, imitate my movements to help you remember the story.**

The Story

The story begins with **Creation** (raise your arms to shoulder height and lower them). God created Adam and Eve so he could have someone to love. But Adam and Eve rebelled against God. Their sin defiled their hearts and the Earth. They caused **Creation** (raise your arms again) to **Fall** (lower your arms).

As men and women populated the Earth they grew more and more rebellious against God. Only one man in all the Earth believed in God and followed God's commands—Noah. So God sent a great **Flood** (use your hands to trickle like rain) that destroyed everything. But God spared Noah and his family.

Years later, one of Noah's descendents, Abraham, became the first citizen of a great nation—Israel. Many years after Abraham died, another nation, Egypt, put the nation of Israel into **Bondage** (clasp your wrists) and made them slaves for 400 years. Finally, God delivered Israel by sending Moses to lead them out of Egypt. Once they left the land of Egypt, they **Wandered** (hold your hand over your eyebrows as though searching) in the desert for 40 years.

Eventually God led Israel to the Promised Land. A rich and beautiful country. But the land was already populated. So, under God's direction, the people of Israel began a **Conquest** (raise one fist in the air). They defeated all the people in the land.

For a long time, the people of Israel had no ruler, and they went through many **Cycles** (draw circles in the air) of obedience and rebellion against God. Finally, God sent them a **King** (bow). That worked well for a while. But the time came when two men fought for Israel's throne, and the kingdom **Split** (make a karate chop with your hand).

From then on, times were tough for God's people. They continued to rebel against God until God sent them into **Exile** (point straight ahead). Foreign nations took God's people captive and carried them away to foreign lands.

After many years, God's people **Returned** (make a beckoning motion) and repopulated the land of Israel. A great **Silence** (say "sshhh" with forefinger in front of your lips) followed when God didn't speak for about 500 years.

And then, **Christ** came (draw a cross in the air) and brought salvation to the world.

The End

Old Testament Progression

Instructions: Make two copies of this sheet and cut the symbols apart as indicated.

CREATION

FALL

FLOOD

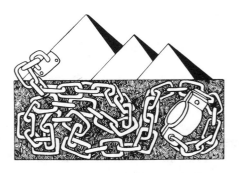

BONDAGE

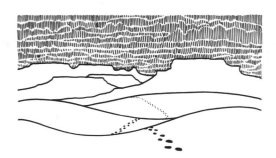

WANDERINGS

CONQUEST

continued

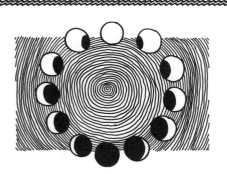

CYCLES

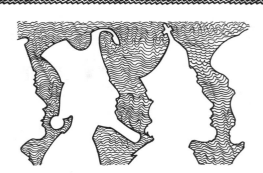

KINGS

SPLIT

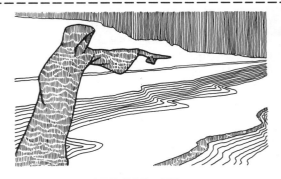

EXILE

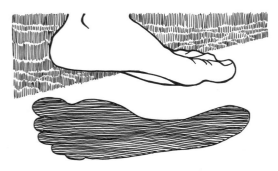

RETURN

SILENCE

CHRIST

Action Covenant

I agree to read three chapters of the Old Testament every week. I also agree to pray daily for God to give me a desire to study the Word and to help me understand it better.

Signed . . . .

Witness . . . .

Date . . . .

God Saw That It Was Good

■ Theme: Appreciating creation (Genesis 1—2)

"And God saw that it was good." These affirming, powerful words come from the earliest part of the scriptures. Genesis 1 and 2 offer two accounts of Creation. In one, humanity is the culminating act of Creation. In the other, God creates humanity first.

This session helps young people understand and appreciate their place in God's creation. It challenges kids to recognize their responsibility as the world's caretakers and encourages them to see their unique value to God.

■ Objectives

During this session participants will:
- read Genesis 1 and 2 and compare the two Creation stories;
- interpret the Creation stories through drama;
- discuss the spiritual truths contained in both stories; and
- covenant to grow in respect and concern for the environment.

■ Preparation

Read and study Genesis 1—2.

You'll need two recordings of the theme song from *2001: A Space Odyssey* (or some other majestic-sounding music) and two tape or record players.

Gather Bibles and pencils. Make a copy of the "Action Covenant" for each person.

The Session

■ Dig

Have group members form a circle and close their eyes. Then read the following guided meditation and pause after each sentence.

Say: **Imagine right now that you could travel to any place in nature that you wanted. Where would that place be? An ocean shore? The mountains? Perhaps a great valley or a crystal blue lake?**

Go to that place in your mind. Relax and enjoy what you see. The air is fresh. The smell of wildflowers and tree blossoms fills your senses. A cool breeze blows in from the west. The clouds roll lazily by, only momentarily blocking the warm, orange sun. As you look around, what do you see? What about this place is special to you?

Now, return to the room and open your eyes.

Ask:

● **Where did you go in your mind? Why?**

● **What about nature is most important to you (trees, water, silence, cool breezes, the fragrance of flowers)? Why?**

■ Discover

Say: **All people want to know how they fit in the "big picture" of our world. Today we're going to study the story of Creation from Genesis 1 and 2. The truths there show us where we fit in God's order and help us see the Earth from a new perspective.**

Form groups of four and have participants discuss:

● Where did God come from?

● What puzzles you about Creation?

● Which is more important to you—how you were created or why you were created? Explain.

● What other questions do you have about Creation?

■ Experience

Form two groups. Assign Genesis 1 to one group and Genesis 2 to the other group. Say: **The first two chapters of Genesis tell about God's Creation. Read the chapter assigned to your group and prepare a silent skit that tells the Creation story. Your group may use the lights and any props here in the room for effect. Use group members to represent different parts of creation, such as trees, animals and people. Assign one group member to control the special effects while the rest perform in the skit.**

I'll play the theme song from *2001: A Space Odyssey* during your performance.

Make sure each group has a Bible, a recording of the theme from *2001: A Space Odyssey* and a tape or record player. Encourage the groups to practice their skits while listening to the music so they can coordinate their pantomime with the sound.

After groups prepare, have them present their skits. Praise their efforts and creativity.

■ Grow

After the skits, gather everyone together and ask:

● **Why does the Bible have two different Creation stories?**

● **What's different about the stories?**

● **How do the two different stories enhance our understanding of Creation?**

Say: **The two Genesis accounts give two unique perspectives on Creation. Genesis 1 gives an overall view of God's creative process, while Genesis 2 focuses on man and woman as the height of God's Creation.**

■ Covenant

Ask:

● **When God gave human beings dominion over the Earth, what do you think he meant?**

● **What attitude do people have toward creation today? In what way does that attitude differ from God's ideal?**

● **Think about the skit you created. Suppose you performed your skit for a friend. What kind of response would you want?**

● **How would you feel if that friend made fun of what you created?**

● **How do you think God feels when the companions he created defile his creation?**

Form groups of four. Then ask: **Briefly, what do Genesis 1 and 2 tell you about yourself and creation?**

After individuals share in their groups, give each person an "Action Covenant" and a pencil. Have kids complete their "Action Covenants" and talk about them in their groups. Tell group members to encourage and pray for each other during the week.

■ Go

Have participants form a circle. Ask them each to think of one part of God's creation they appreciate. Close the session by asking each person to complete this prayer: "God, thank you for creating . . ." When everyone is finished, have a moment of silence and say: **Amen**.

Action Covenant

Because God loves me, he has given me this world to care for and enjoy. To fulfill my calling as a caretaker of the Earth, I agree to do two of the following (circle two):

1. *Spend more time in nature by going to the park weekly or taking up a hobby that involves nature.*

2. *Pick up litter when I see it—wherever I see it.*

3. *Read about environmental issues that face our world, and take action to stop a problem. (For instance, write a letter to my state or federal representative, or donate money to an environmental cause.)*

4. *Stop littering.*

5. *Other:* _____

Signed . . . .
Witness . . . .
Date . . . .

Don't Buy the Lie!

■ Theme: Resisting temptation (Genesis 3)

Genesis 3 provides a choice example of the cunning subtlety of temptation. The story of the Fall illustrates that despite God's plan for a good creation, human beings choose to disobey their creator and alienate themselves from him.

When Adam and Eve decided to eat the forbidden fruit—to make the rules, to engineer life, to control their destinies, to "play God"— they encountered disaster.

This session encourages kids to discuss openly the temptations in their lives and shows them how to fight the urge to sin.

■ Objectives

During this session participants will:
- read Genesis 3 and discuss its symbolism;
- discuss the dangers inherent in temptation;
- list the temptations they face in their lives; and
- covenant to work on one particular temptation.

■ Preparation

Read and study Genesis 3.

Gather a Bible and pencil for each participant. Make a copy of the "How It All Started" handout and the "Action Covenant" for each person.

Divide the room into five sections. For each section, gather scissors, glue, markers, posterboard and a stack of magazines and newspapers.

The Session

■ Dig

Form a group around each set of magazines, newspapers and other supplies. Say: **Cut or tear pictures that illustrate temptations from the magazines and newspapers. Glue your examples on the posterboard to make a collage. For example, you might use a picture of a dollar bill to illustrate how greed tempts people. Use your imagination. Use the markers to draw illustrations or label collages.**

Have all groups meet together and present their collages.

■ Discover

Ask participants to remain in their groups. Give each person a copy of the "How It All Started" handout. Assign each group one of the following parts: Narrator, God, Adam, Eve or Serpent. Say: **This reading is based on Genesis 2—3 and focuses on the temptation of Adam and Eve.**

After the reading, assign a corner of the room for each of the three characters—Adam, Eve and the Serpent. Have people each stand in the corner that best represents their answer to each of the following:

● **Who's the worst character in this story?**

● **Which character was least responsible for causing sin to enter God's creation?**

Each time ask the people in each corner to discuss why they chose that answer.

■ Experience

While kids are still in their corner groups, say: **When people do things wrong, they often blame others for their failings. Think of three reasons why each of the other two characters might be more to blame than your character. Plan your arguments so your character appears the most innocent. For example, the Eve group might say that Eve wasn't to blame because the Serpent suggested the whole thing and then Adam encouraged her. Use your imagination.**

After groups plan their arguments, stage a debate over who's most responsible for sin entering God's creation.

■ Grow

After the debate, form one circle and ask:

● **Did anyone win the debate? Why or why not?**
● **Why does God allow people to sin? to make their own decisions?**
● **In what ways do you or people you know act like Adam and Eve?**

Have a volunteer read aloud Genesis 3:14-19. Ask:
● **How is sin related to physical suffering?**
● **Is suffering a punishment for sin or a result of sin?**

■ Covenant

Form groups of three. Give kids each a pencil and an "Action Covenant." Have them discuss in their groups the temptations they face and how they can overcome those temptations. Then instruct them to each complete the "Action Covenant."

■ Go

Divide the group into the original five groups. Give each group its collage. Have group members each look at the collage and find a picture that represents one temptation they've asked God to help them overcome.

Close with this prayer: **God, there are so many temptations. Remind us to rely on you to help us say no when we feel tempted. Fill us with your Holy Spirit to help us resist when we want to give in and not do your will. In Jesus' name, amen.**

Have the groups rip up the collages.

How It All Started

Instructions: Read your part aloud. If you're reading with a group, try to sound like one voice as you read together.

Narrator: The Lord God took the man and put him in the Garden of Eden to work it and take care of it. And the Lord God commanded the man,

God: You are free to eat from any tree in the garden; but you must not eat from the tree of the knowledge of good and evil, for when you eat of it you will surely die.

Narrator: The Lord God said,

God: It is not good for the man to be alone. I will make a helper suitable for him.

Narrator: Now the Lord God had formed out of the ground all the beasts of the field and all the birds of the air. He brought them to the man to see what he would name them; and whatever the man called each living creature, that was its name. So the man gave names to all the livestock, the birds of the air and all the beasts of the field.

But for Adam no suitable helper was found. So the Lord God caused the man to fall into a deep sleep; and while he was sleeping, he took one of the man's ribs and closed up the place with flesh.

Then the Lord God made a woman from the rib he had taken out of the man, and he brought her to the man. The man said,

Adam: This is now bone of my bones and flesh of my flesh; she shall be called "woman," for she was taken out of man.

Narrator: The man and his wife were both naked, and they felt no shame.

Now the serpent was more crafty than any of the wild animals the Lord God had made. He said to the woman,

Serpent: (Sly, questioning voice) Did God really say, "You must not eat from any tree in the garden"?

continued

Eve: (Firmly) We may eat fruit from the trees in the garden, but God did say, "You must not eat fruit from the tree that is in the middle of the garden, and you must not touch it, or you will die."

Serpent: (Emphatic statement of assurance) You will not surely die. For God knows that when you eat of it your eyes will be opened, and you will be like God, knowing good and evil.

Narrator: When the woman saw that the fruit of the tree was good for food and pleasing to the eye, and also desirable for gaining wisdom, she took some and ate it. She also gave some to her husband, who was with her, and he ate it.

Then the eyes of both of them were opened, and they realized they were naked; so they sewed fig leaves together and made coverings for themselves.

Then the man and his wife heard the sound of the Lord God as he was walking in the garden in the cool of the day, and they hid from the Lord God among the trees of the garden. But the Lord God called to the man,

God: Where are you?

Adam: (Apologetic) I heard you in the garden, and I was afraid because I was naked; so I hid.

God: Who told you that you were naked? Have you eaten from the tree that I commanded you not to eat from?

Adam: (Blaming) The woman you put here with me—she gave me some fruit from the tree, and I ate it.

God: (To Eve) What is this you have done?

Eve: (Blaming) The serpent deceived me, and I ate.

Adapted from The Holy Bible, New International Version.

Action Covenant

Two temptations I'm facing in my life right now are . . .

"No temptation has seized you except what is common to man. And God is faithful; he will not let you be tempted beyond what you can bear. But when you are tempted, he will also provide a way out so that you can stand up under it" (1 Corinthians 10:13).

One "way out" God has provided for each of these temptations is . . .

I agree to pray for myself and my group members this week for God to help us overcome these temptations in our lives.

> *Signed* . . . .
> *Witness* . . . .
> *Date* . . . .

Walls of Sin

■ Theme: Facing sin's alienation (Genesis 4—11)

Genesis 4—11 describes a destructive spiral that brings hopelessness unless God intervenes. These chapters illustrate how sin alienates us from God, each other and the world.

We experience alienation from each other in the same way Adam and Eve felt the shame of their nakedness. We experience alienation from God in the same way the first couple hid from God in the garden. And we experience the alienation of nation against nation in the same way people did at the Tower of Babel.

This session helps young people talk openly about sin and how it alienates us from God and others. This session will also help kids understand sin's effects and the cost of God's forgiveness.

■ Objectives

During this session participants will:
- explore Genesis 4—11;
- discuss ways they feel alienation in different areas of their lives;
- read and discuss incidents of alienation found in Genesis 4—11;
- experience how sin's alienation affects their relationship with God; and
- discover ways to overcome alienation in their lives.

■ Preparation

Read and study Genesis 4—11.

Gather newsprint, masking tape, markers, construction paper, paper and Bibles.

Write each of the following phrases on a separate sheet of newsprint, and tape one sheet on each wall of the room:
- between you and classmates
- between you and your parents
- between nations of the world
- between yourself and God

Write each of the following on separate sheets of construction paper. Then tape sheets on one wall. Tape a long sheet of newsprint below the scripture passages.

1. Genesis 4:2b-16   **3.** Genesis 9:1-7
2. Genesis 6:11-13; 20-22   **4.** Genesis 11:1-9

The Session

■ Dig

Ask group members each to stand next to the sheet of newsprint that reflects the relationship they feel the most alienation in right now. Give each person a marker. Then say: **The people around you are struggling with the same kind of alienation you are. Tell the others around you what causes the alienation you feel. Then write your response on the newsprint. For example, you might say, ''I feel alienated because my dad is always away on business trips.''**

After everyone has responded, gather everyone together and discuss each group's comments.

■ Discover

Give each person paper, a pencil and a Bible. Number off the group by fours. Say: **All of us have experienced alienation. We know what it's like to feel separated from others. Genesis 4—11 illustrates what happens when sin's alienation gains momentum.**

Refer to the passages on the wall and have kids each look up the scripture assigned to their number. Have kids read their assigned passages and list the incidents of alienation on their papers. After kids work a few minutes alone, instruct those who were assigned the same scripture passage to work in a group to find more incidents of alienation. After about five minutes, ask:

● **How did you feel when you were trying to do the assignment on your own?**

● **How did your feelings change when you got to work with others?**

Ask each group to share with the others the incidents of alienation it found in its scripture passage. Then ask:

● **How would you sum up the message of Genesis 4—11 in only three words?** List responses on the long sheet of newsprint.

Then discuss:

● **How are we like the characters in the scripture passages you just studied?**

● **Why does sin cause alienation?**

● **In what way does God work in our lives to overcome the alienation sin brings?**

■ Experience

Instruct each group to form a circle with an open Bible at its center. Say: **Explore feelings of alienation while I take you through** an experience. **Remain quiet through the experience so you can hear me clearly and follow my instructions. Begin by looking at the open Bible in the center of your circle.**

Read aloud the scripture printed in the box titled "Separation." After reading each portion, instruct the group to move or act as indicated. Instruct kids to maintain the position you tell them to get into until you give the next instruction or until someone touches them to indicate that the experience is over. (You might want to have another leader give the italicized instructions.)

■ Grow

Gather everyone in one circle and ask:

● **What did you feel as you heard the scripture read?**

● **How did you feel about not being able to hear the entire message?**

● **How is this experience like the alienation between us and God when we sin?**

● **When someone touched you to let you know the experience was over, how did you feel?**

● **How was someone touching you like what happens when God forgives us?**

Tell the group you read more scripture while their ears were covered. Read aloud the last section from the box again (Isaiah 1:18, 19, 20c). Then ask:

● **How does sin prevent you from hearing God speak?**

● **What can you do to break through the walls of alienation caused by sin?**

● **If you did break down the walls of alienation, how would your life change?**

■ Go

Ask young people each to sit silently somewhere in the room, away from other group members. Turn out the lights. Make sure the room is completely dark. If you can't darken the room completely, have kids close their eyes.

Pause a moment, then say: **Alienation happens when you feel isolated or detached from God and those around you. Think of a time in the past week that you felt isolated and why.**

With the lights still out or eyes still closed, have each person tell about a time of alienation.

Say: **God is our only hope in our struggle against the alienation of sin. We can't fully escape this alienation because it's part of living in this world. But through Christ's power we're no longer captive to sin. We can say no to sin's power when we work with Christ to tear down the walls of alienation in our lives.**

Close with the following prayer: **God, your love for us is greater than our sin. Help us trust in your love for us and the power of your Holy Spirit to change us. For it is through your power that we can face life victoriously. In Jesus' name, amen.**

Separation

Surely the arm of the Lord is not too short to save, nor his ear too dull to hear. But your iniquities have separated you from your God;

Turn around with your backs to each other.

So justice is far from us, and righteousness does not reach us. We look for light but all is darkness; for brightness, but we walk in deep shadows.

Close your eyes.

Like the blind we grope along the wall, feeling our way like men without eyes.

Take one step away from the circle.

For our offenses are many in your sight, and our sins testify against us . . . rebellion and treachery against the Lord, turning our backs on our God,

Take another step away from the circle.

uttering lies our hearts have conceived . . . Truth is nowhere to be found,

Hum softly to yourself.

The Lord looked and was displeased that there was no justice.

Cover your ears tightly.

Come now, let us reason together, says the Lord. Though your sins are like scarlet, they shall be as white as snow; though they are red as crimson, they shall be like wool. If you are willing and obedient, you will eat the best from the land . . . the mouth of the Lord has spoken.

(Not spoken) When you're finished reading, touch one young person from each group and have him or her touch others to indicate that the experience is over.

Verses selected from Isaiah 59:1-15 and Isaiah 1:18-20, NIV.

A Noble Beginning

■ Theme: Building faith (Genesis 12)

In Genesis 12 God called Abram to father a nation. But Abram's wife was childless and beyond childbearing age. Abram's life gives young people an example of someone who leaves everything behind—simply because of God's command.

This session focuses on faith. It targets the way God summons people to leave the safety and security of their lives to follow him in faith. This study encourages young people to follow God's leading and discover what faith means in their lives.

■ Objectives

During this session participants will:
- read Genesis 12;
- talk about faith and how it affects people's lives;
- plot Abram's journey on a map;
- take faith journeys and talk about faith;
- acknowledge personal faith characteristics; and
- covenant to work on a way to strengthen their faith.

■ Preparation

Read and study Genesis 12.

Record interviews with several people in your congregation or community. Ask, "What was the greatest risk you ever took by faith?"

Gather a cassette player, masking tape, newsprint, markers, pencils, Bibles and paper. Find a whistle, bell or some other noisemaker to use in the Experience section.

Tape one sheet of newsprint on the wall. Write the word "Faith" on the top.

Write "Let go and let God" on a piece of paper. Tape it inside the lid of a small suitcase.

Make one copy of the "Map of Abram's Journey" handout and "Action Covenant" for each person. For every four people: make one copy of the "Faith Journeys" handout. Cut the "Faith Journeys" into four sections as indicated. Insert the four sections and three bandannas in a large brown envelope.

The Session

■ Dig

Gather everyone in a circle. Play the recorded interviews.

Ask:

- **What do these people believe about God?**
- **How does their faith influence their actions?**

List responses on newsprint.

■ Discover

Say: **Today we're exploring Genesis 12. We meet Abram, a man picked by God to bless the entire world. Let's learn about the life journey of this person who's not really so different from you and me.**

Form groups of four. Give each small group a copy of the "Map of Abram's Journey" handout, a pencil and a Bible. Have groups follow the instructions on the handout.

Then ask: **How would you have responded to God's command to "Leave your country . . . and go to the land I will show you"?**

■ Experience

Ask group members to remain in their groups. Say: **Each group will take four faith journeys. Take turns being the leader. When you're the leader, take one set of directions from the "Faith Journeys" packet. If you're the first leader, take the Journey One directions; if you're the second leader, take the Journey Two directions, and so on. Read the instructions to yourself and follow them. Don't tell the group where you're going. You'll have seven minutes to complete each journey and the discussion. Listen for the signal to change leaders.**

Demonstrate the signal (a whistle, bell, or other noisemaker) so kids will know what sound to expect.

Once all groups have completed their journeys, ask:

- **What feelings did you experience in your journeys?**
- **Which of these feelings do you think Abram experienced? Give examples.**
- **Why is faith important? Give an example of how faith makes a difference in people's lives.**

■ Grow

Gather everyone in a circle. Give each person a pencil and paper. Ask: **If God needed something done right this moment and called you to do it, what faith qualities do you have that would help you get the job done? Write these on your paper.**

After kids make their lists, have them talk about faith qualities they have that could help them do a good job.

■ Covenant

Give each person an "Action Covenant." Ask kids each to complete the covenant and talk with one other person in the circle about what they wrote.

■ Go

Hold up the suitcase. Say: **In this suitcase is what Abram found faith really means. What do you think is in this suitcase?** After a few responses, open the suitcase to reveal the "Let go and let God" sign.

Ask:

- **What does this statement mean to you?**
- **How can you do this in your own life?**

Have someone read John 3:16. Ask: **How does this scripture relate to the statement "Let go and let God"?**

Ask each person to complete this sentence prayer: "God, thank you for giving me the faith to . . ."

Map of Abram's Journey

Instructions: Read Genesis 11:31-32; 12:1, 4-10. Plot Abram's journey from Ur to Egypt. Then answer the questions.

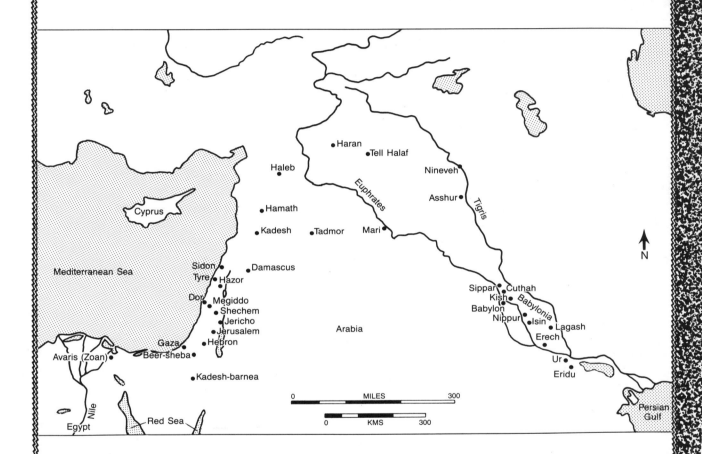

1. How far did Abram travel?_____

_____

2. Who did Abram take with him? _____

_____

Faith Journeys

Instructions: Cut the "Faith Journeys" into four sections as indicated. Make a copy for each group of four.

✂ -

Leader for Faith Journey One:

1. Choose a location within the meeting room. Lead group members to that location.

2. Discuss: If you had been Abram, what three questions would you have wanted God to answer before you began your journey?

- -

Leader for Faith Journey Two:

1. Choose any location within the building. Ask group members to hold hands. Lead them to that location.

2. Discuss: What people (adults and young people) do you know who have a strong faith? Give an example of their faith in action.

- -

Leader for Faith Journey Three:

1. Choose a site outside the building. Have group members line up behind you. Ask them each to close their eyes, hold on to the shoulders of the person in front of them and follow you to the location. Ask group members not to talk throughout the journey.

2. Discuss: What recent experience caused you to take a risk totally on faith? How did it work out? Why?

- -

Leader for Faith Journey Four:

1. Have group members line up behind you. Stand at the front of the line with three bandannas. Hold the end of one bandanna with your right hand and give a bandanna to each of the two people directly behind you. Tell them each to hold the end of their bandanna with their right hand. Ask group members each to reach with their left hand and take hold of the bandanna directly in front of them. This should link the group together in a line.

Ask group members to close their eyes, hang on to the bandannas and listen to your directions while you lead them back to the original meeting place. Warn group members about anything that might cause them to stumble.

2. Discuss: Which of these faith journeys required the most faith? Why?

Action Covenant

One area of my life in which God is calling me to strengthen my faith is . . .

To build my faith in that area this week I'll . . .

Signed: . . . .
Witness: . . . .
Date: . . . .

Favored to Forgive

■ Theme: Receiving forgiveness (Genesis 37—45)

Genesis 37—45 describes the later years of Jacob's life. Intrigue and drama highlighted these years as the focus changed to Jacob's son Joseph. Joseph's status as the favored child turned out to be a curse when his jealous brothers cunningly sold him into slavery.

If anyone was entitled to a grudge, it was Joseph. Yet through spiritual discipline, Joseph maintained his faith in God's guidance and forgave his brothers.

This session illustrates for young people the faith and forgiveness God asks of each of us.

■ Objectives

During this session participants will:
- scan Genesis 37—45 and discuss the events in Joseph's life;
- discuss how unforgiveness affects their lives;
- examine their own attitudes toward forgiveness; and
- experience the freedom of forgiveness.

■ Preparation

Read and study Genesis 37—45.

Gather a brick and marker for each participant. You'll need newsprint, masking tape, chalkboard, chalk, eraser, Bibles and pencils. Make a copy of the "Choices About Forgiveness" handout for each person.

Write each of the following open-ended statements on a separate sheet of newsprint and tape sheets on the wall:
- Forgiveness means . . .
- I have a hard time forgiving my friends when they . . .
- It's hard to forgive my parents when they . . .
- I have trouble forgiving my teachers when they . . .
- I have difficulty forgiving myself when I . . .

The Session

■ Dig

Give group members each a marker and a brick. Tell them they must carry their bricks and markers until you tell them what to do with them.

Have group members use their markers to write responses—on the newsprint—to the open-ended statements.

After kids write their responses, gather everyone in a circle. Remind kids to keep their bricks and markers. Have kids read and discuss the responses.

Then ask:

What's one thing someone could do to you that you couldn't forgive?

List at least 10 ideas on the chalkboard.

■ Discover

Form four groups. Give kids each a Bible and remind them to keep their bricks and markers with them. Assign each group one of the following scripture passages:

- Genesis 37:2-4, 23-36
- Genesis 39:1-3, 6-20
- Genesis 41:39-43
- Genesis 42:1-5; 45:1-7

Say: **Joseph's life demonstrates how a person can forgive others—even his relatives. Read the scripture passage assigned to your group and pick out the ways others wronged Joseph and how he responded. When every group is finished, we'll talk about what you found.**

After all the groups share their discoveries, ask:

- **What's the most significant thing you learned about Joseph from these scriptures?**
- **How did God seem to fail Joseph?**
- **Why did Joseph continue to trust God even when God seemed to fail him?**
- **If you were in Joseph's place, how would you have responded to the people who harmed you?**
- **How would you have responded to God?**

■ Experience

Ask:

How did it feel to carry your brick all this time?

Encourage people to talk about specific times when carrying the brick was difficult.

Say: **On your brick write something someone has done to you that's difficult to forgive.**

Then ask:

● **How is carrying a brick like not forgiving someone?**

● **Now that you've written on your brick, how do you feel about others seeing it?**

● **What would you like to do with your brick? Why?**

Have group members pair up to talk about what they wrote on their bricks. Make sure each person has a partner.

After a few minutes, say: **Think about how you can help your partner get rid of his or her brick. You might cover your partner's brick with a cloth. Without speaking, decide what you want to do with your partner's brick and do it. You have one minute.**

After everyone is finished, have partners talk about their actions and how they felt about what the other person did with their brick. Then call everyone back together. Allow kids to lay their bricks on the floor. Ask:

● **How did your partner's action represent an attempt at forgiveness?**

● **What do you do when you forgive someone?**

● **What would Jesus have done with your brick?**

● **What would Jesus do with the list of things we've written on the chalkboard?**

■ Grow

Give each person a pencil and a "Choices About Forgiveness" handout. Say: **All of us have had to choose whether to forgive someone. Joseph had to make a hard choice about forgiving his brothers. For his family, this was a life or death decision because he had the food the family needed. This handout asks you to think about forgiveness in various situations.**

After everyone has completed the handout, have kids each find a new partner and discuss:

What did you learn about your feelings on forgiveness?

Once all partners have had a chance to speak, say: **Joseph was a great man, yet he still needed God's forgiveness for his sin. Think about an area of your life in which you need God's forgiveness. Share that area with your partner; then pray for each other.**

■ Go

Ask group members to bring their bricks and form a circle. Read aloud Ephesians 4:31-32. Say: **Forgiving someone is easy to talk about but hard to do. God calls each of us to put forgiveness to**

work so we can have a richer life.

With God's forgiveness, there's no residue. He doesn't keep track of how many times he forgives. He erases the board and wipes it clean. And we need to follow his example.

Erase the chalkboard. Ask each person to think of a person he or she needs to forgive. Tell kids each to imagine that the brick is that person's offense. Have individuals take turns placing their bricks in the circle's center to form a cross. Ask young people each to say the word "forgiven" as they put the brick in place.

Have group members each close their eyes and think about the person they need to forgive as you read the following suggestions:

- **Don't be afraid to admit you're hurting.**
- **Realize forgiveness isn't impossible. It *can* take place.**
- **Forgive and let go. Turn your anger or pain over to God, and let him do the rest. Forgiveness can happen. God's Spirit can work in both people's lives to heal the relationship.**

Ask the group to pray silently that God will help them be forgiving.

Choices About Forgiveness

Instructions: Circle the choice that reflects how you feel about each statement.

1. I should always forgive, no matter what the circumstance.　　Yes　No

2. Some things should never be forgiven.　　Yes　No

3. Joseph had every right not to forgive his brothers.　　Yes　No

4. I know people I can't forgive.　　Yes　No

5. I know people who can't forgive me.　　Yes　No

6. I'm the kind of person who holds a grudge for a while before I forgive.　　Yes　No

7. God forgives too easily.　　Yes　No

8. I have a hard time forgiving myself when I hurt someone.　　Yes　No

9. I could do things that God wouldn't forgive.　　Yes　No

10. Our world is messed up because we don't understand forgiveness' power.　　Yes　No

11. I find it difficult to forgive my parents when they make a mistake.　　Yes　No

12. I expect others to apologize before I forgive them.　　Yes　No

The Stubborn Pharaoh

■ Theme: Being persistent (Exodus 7—14)

In Exodus 7—14, God sent Moses to deliver God's people. Moses dared to tell the stubborn Pharaoh, "Let my people go." Yet many wondered about this representative from the God, Yahweh, who dared to tangle with the ruler of Egypt. One disaster after another failed to motivate the mighty Pharaoh to release Israel. Then God dealt the final blow. After listening to Pharaoh's refusals, God killed the firstborn in each household but "passed over" the marked homes of the Israelites. While Pharaoh suffered because of his arrogance, the Israelites moved quickly out of their enslavement.

Moses was persistent. His stubborn faith refused to be shaken by his dismal circumstances.

This session will help young people wrestle with their problems and discover their need for persistent faith.

■ Objectives

During this session participants will:
- discuss the important events in Exodus 7—14;
- explore the theme of persistence in a simulation activity; and
- identify the presence or absence of persistence in their lives.

■ Preparation

Read and study Exodus 7—14.

Collect three or four news articles about recent natural disasters (such as earthquakes, floods or violent storms). Find articles that deal with how these disasters affected the people involved.

Gather Bibles, a deck of cards (3×5 cards will also work), newsprint and markers for each small group. You will also need a prize for the winning team during the Experience section.

The Session

■ Dig

Show the group the natural-disaster articles. Briefly explain the events in each one. Then summarize what happened in Egypt during the plagues. Ask:

Which plague would have been hardest for you to experience? Why?

■ Discover

Form five groups. Each group needs a least two people. (If you have fewer than 10 people, cut the role play of Exodus 14. Or give two scripture sections to one group.) Give each group a Bible. Say: **Exodus 7—14 describes the great power struggle between Moses and Pharaoh, and the final departure of the Israelites from Egypt.**

Assign each group one of the following scripture passages:

- Exodus 7—8
- Exodus 9—10
- Exodus 11—12:30
- Exodus 12:31—13:22
- Exodus 14

Have groups each prepare a role play of the text as if group members were the characters. Tell groups that everyone must play a part. Encourage kids to be creative. For instance, they may want to set the story in modern-day New York City or use British accents. Be certain the groups stay true to the text's general content.

After all groups have role-played their stories, ask:

- **What struggle is going on in these passages?**
- **Why is Pharaoh so arrogant?**
- **If you had been in Pharaoh's position, how would you have reacted to Moses?**

■ Experience

Have kids stay in their groups. Hand each group a deck of cards. Say: **One thing we see in all of these passages is Moses' persistence. All of us face difficult situations. "Hanging in there" through rough times is sometimes tough to do.**

Work together in your group to build a tower with these cards. Use as many cards as you can. You'll have 10 minutes to complete your task.

When time is up, give a prize to the group that built the highest structure. Bring all kids together and ask:

- **What was the most difficult part of this task?**

- **When did you get frustrated? Why?**
- **What did this project have to do with persistence?**
- **Why is it so natural to want to give up?**

■ Grow

Have kids meet in groups of four. Say: **It's impossible to accomplish much without staying power. People who aspire to be great athletes must work hard through years of training. Likewise, Moses had to be persistent with Pharaoh to get results. How has persistence worked for you? Explain the situation to your group.**

After everyone has shared an experience, ask:

- **When did you finally give up on something and quit? What did you learn from the experience? Talk about the experience in your groups.**

After groups have discussed giving up, gather the groups together and talk about their responses. Then ask:

- **Why was Moses so persistent?**
- **In what situations are you most persistent?**
- **The Israelites began to doubt when they saw the chariots. How does doubt affect your ability to endure rough times?**
- **How did the Israelites know God was with them? How do you know God is present in your life?**
- **What does faith have to do with persistence?**

■ Go

Read aloud John 15:26-27. Ask:

How does God's Holy Spirit work in our lives to help us endure?

Tell everyone to find a partner. Then say: **Think about one area of your life in which you need more persistence. Discuss with your partner how you can help each other become more persistent. You may decide to pray for each other. Or you may want to be accountable to each other concerning the problem area.**

Ask group members each to complete this sentence prayer for their partner: "God, give my partner the persistence to . . . And give me the persistence to help." When everyone has finished, say: **Amen.**

Foundations for Living

■ Theme: Understanding rules (Exodus 19—24)

Exodus 19—24 describes the Israelites' arrival at Mount Sinai. This was a scene of unforgettable blessing. Moses consecrated the people and readied them to receive God's covenant law. God spoke and gave this infant nation its foundation for living. The Ten Commandments were etched in tablets of stone, and the covenant law was sealed by blood.

This session centers around rules—a hot topic for teenagers. Young people sometimes react strongly to rules. This session helps them understand that rules are critical to life.

■ Objectives

During this session participants will:
● explore the events of Exodus 19—24;
● discuss the laws given to the Israelites at Mount Sinai;
● create new commandments of love for their lives; and
● covenant to strengthen their obedience to one of the Ten Commandments.

■ Preparation

Read and study Exodus 19—24.

Gather Bibles, newsprint, markers and pencils. Make a copy of the handout "The 10 Commandments of Love" and the "Action Covenant" for each person.

Make a 3-foot A on one sheet of newsprint, and a 3-foot B on another. Tape these letters on opposite ends of one wall.

The Session

■ Dig

Explain that you've set up a continuum along one wall. Ask kids to stand anywhere between A and B, depending on how they feel about the two choices for each statement. Read these statements or create your own. Pause after each statement and have kids explain their choices.

1. Faith in God is more like:
   A. keeping the rules; or
   B. freedom of choice.
2. Without laws for our society, we would:
   A. become more civilized; or
   B. become less civilized.
3. Rules at school should be:
   A. always open to change; or
   B. set by the administration and strictly enforced.
4. Laws should be made by:
   A. a vote of the public; or
   B. individuals who have the greatest knowledge.
5. Rules in the family should:
   A. be voted on by all family members; or
   B. be made by parents after a family discussion.

■ Discover

Say: **When the Israelites left Egypt, they still suffered the effects of slavery—they didn't know how to relate as free men and women. They needed a framework for living. That's why God brought them to Mount Sinai.**

Today we'll explore the Mount Sinai experience and examine the laws God established. We want to see what it means to be his people. But first, let's look at what led to the experience at Mount Sinai.

Form three groups. Assign three of the following passages to each group:

- Exodus 20:1-17
- Exodus 20:21-26
- Exodus 21:1-11
- Exodus 21:12-17
- Exodus 21:18-35
- Exodus 22:1-15
- Exodus 22:16-31
- Exodus 23:1-9
- Exodus 23:10-19a

Give each group newsprint and a marker. Say: **These passages contain the laws given to Israel. As a group, read your passages and write the law you feel is most important and the law you feel is least important.**

■ Experience

After groups have finished, say: **Now make a people-sculpture illustrating the law your group decided was most important. For example, one group might illustrate "You shall not murder" by demonstrating a murder scene, then having one group member form an "X" in front of the scene. Use your imagination to design your sculpture.**

While groups plan, tape newsprint on the wall. Have groups present their people-sculptures and list the laws as they're demonstrated. Then ask:

- **How do you feel about the laws God gave to Israel?**
- **Which ones seemed unfair?**
- **Why did God give Israel laws?**
- **If you had been one of the Israelites, how would you have felt after you heard these laws?**
- **How do you feel now when people give you rules?**

■ Grow

Ask participants to select a partner. Give each pair the handout "The 10 Commandments of Love." Say: **With your partner, choose 10 critical ingredients of love. Write 10 new commandments we should use to govern our lives. Base your new commandments on what you know about the Christian faith. For example, you might write "You shall be kind to everyone you meet." You may want to use 1 Corinthians 13 as a foundation.**

While pairs are working, tape a sheet of newsprint on the wall next to the list of important laws your kids chose earlier. When pairs are finished, have them share their new commandments with the rest of the group. List these new commandments on the newsprint. Then ask:

- **What differences do you notice between your commandments and God's commandments? Are both sets of commandments based on love? Explain your answer.**
- **Which new commandment is hardest for you to keep? Why?**
- **Look at the new commandments. Which ones are most Christlike? Which ones aren't Christlike?**
- **Why is it easy to forget God's laws?**

■ Covenant

Have volunteers read aloud Exodus 20:1-17, one verse at a time. Give each person an "Action Covenant" and have kids complete their covenants. Form a circle and have kids each share what they wrote.

■ Go

Remain in the circle. Read aloud Exodus 17:8-15. Say: **The Israelites were successful against the Amalekites as long as Moses had his arms lifted in submission to God. Let's hold hands and lift our arms together as we pray to the source of our strength.**

Pray: **God, scripture says that your Word is tested seven times and found pure. Sometimes we forget the Ten Commandments and think they had value only during Moses' time. Remind us of the importance of your laws today. Help us uphold your laws and show others that your commandments are still holy. In Jesus' name, amen.**

The 10 Commandments of Love

Instructions: On the tablets below, write 10 new commandments of love that begin with the words "You shall." These commandments should reflect how you feel God wants you to apply love in your daily life.

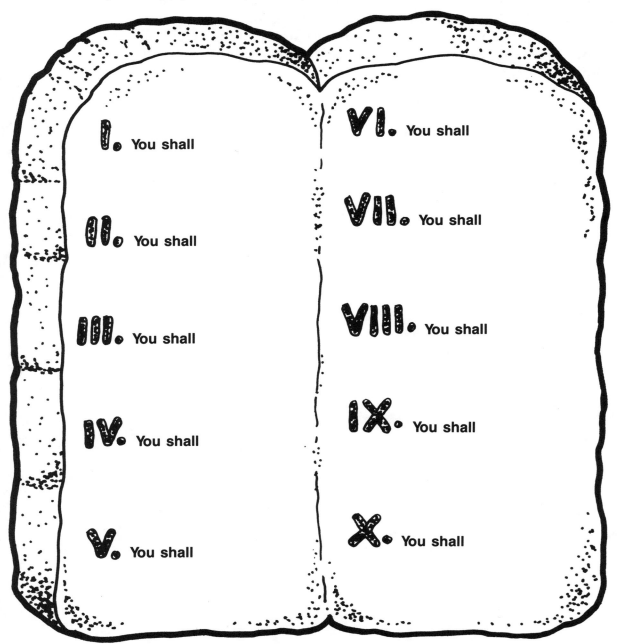

I. You shall

II. You shall

III. You shall

IV. You shall

V. You shall

VI. You shall

VII. You shall

VIII. You shall

IX. You shall

X. You shall

Action Covenant

The commandment I need to work on most is . . .

To follow that commandment more closely, I will covenant to . . .

Signed . . . .

Witness . . . .

Date . . . .

Grace 101

■ Theme: Growing in grace (Leviticus)

"Leviticus" literally means "pertaining to the Levites." It's filled with laws concerning the priesthood and the people's conduct. The book's center contains a powerful chapter that discloses God's grace. Atonement became God's gift by which sin could be forgiven. In the fabric of Levitical moral and ceremonial guidelines, God's grace began to unfold.

In their search for independence, teenagers struggle constantly with regulations. They also have difficulty understanding mistakes—not only others', but their own. This session explores the struggle to understand God's law and discover God's forgiveness.

■ Objectives

During this session participants will:
● review the book of Leviticus and discuss Israel's laws;
● put Israel's laws into a contemporary context;
● covenant to get rid of one "scapegoat" in their lives; and
● experience atonement as a gift of God's grace.

■ Preparation

Scan the book of Leviticus, and study closely chapter 16.

Gather newsprint, markers, candles, candleholders, matches, masking tape, Bibles, pencils, paper, three grocery sacks, 3×5 cards, thumbtacks and a portable wooden cross.

Into each of the three sacks place: one yard of ribbon, a dime, pencil, paper clip, sock, drinking cup and crayon.

Make a copy of the "Action Covenant" for each person.

The Session

■ Dig

Form groups of four. Give each group newsprint, a marker, a candle in a candleholder, and matches. Ask each group to light its candle. Then darken the room. Say: **Your worst fears have been realized. While you were at school, the world was ravaged by a nuclear war. You and your classmates survived in a shelter. You're all that's left of our once great society.**

One task you face in starting over and developing your new society is to write laws. Within your groups, write five basic laws that would preserve your society and keep it civilized. For example, one law might be "All criminal acts will be punished by death."

After 10 minutes, turn on the lights and ask groups to blow out their candles. Bring everyone together. Have a volunteer from each group tape the group's list of laws on the wall and read them aloud. Then ask:

- **Was it difficult to decide on five laws? Why or why not?**
- **What criteria did you use?**
- **Do your five laws cover everything? Why or why not?**
- **What would happen without laws?**

■ Discover

Say: **The book of Leviticus contains the moral and ceremonial laws for the Israelites. All the laws God gave at Mount Sinai are collected in this book. Chapters 1—7 contain the laws and rituals for worship. Chapters 8—10 include the laws concerning priests. Chapters 11—15 contain the laws for purification. And Chapter 16, the highlight of the book, gives the details for the Day of Atonement.**

Give each person a Bible, pencil and paper. Form four groups (a group may be as small as one). Assign each group one of these scripture passages:

- Leviticus 15:1-18
- Leviticus 12 and 15:19-30
- Leviticus 18
- Leviticus 20 and 24

Have group members each read their verses and list five laws from their scripture passage that would be controversial today.

When groups are ready, have them take turns reading their controversial laws to the other groups. As they read each law, have everyone give a thumbs-up or thumbs-down vote on whether our society should have that law today.

■ Experience

Form three groups. Divide the following topics among the groups—sexual conduct, personal conduct, and punishments. Hand each group one of the sacks you've prepared and say: **Using all the objects in your sack, design a mime presentation for your topic. Your skit should communicate how you would rewrite the Levitical laws to make them more contemporary.**

For example, I've put a ribbon in your sack. The personal-conduct group might have two people hold on to the ends of the ribbon to communicate being bound by God's love instead of by law. The sexual-conduct group might tie a guy's and girl's wrists together with the ribbon to communicate the sacredness of sex in marriage. The punishments group might tie the ribbon around a rolled-up piece of paper as a symbol of a law that entitles everyone to a trial by jury. Remember to use all the objects in the sack.

Give 10 minutes for groups to plan their mime presentations. Have groups meet together and share their creativity.

■ Grow

Say: **God gave his people a way to release themselves from sin's burden and bondage. Turn to Leviticus 16.**

Go around the group, having each person read a verse. After the reading, ask:

● **Had you heard the term "scapegoat" before? How do these verses explain that term?**

● **What does "scapegoat" mean to you?**

● **Why do we often blame someone or something else for our mistakes?**

● **Have you or someone close to you ever been used as a scapegoat? How did it feel?**

● **What is atonement?**

● **Without atonement, what do you think would've happened to Israel? Why?**

Read aloud 2 Corinthians 5:21. Say: **Things changed dramatically when Jesus came. He became the final scapegoat, the ultimate sacrifice. No longer are we held in bondage to our sin.**

■ Covenant

Read aloud Romans 5:6-11. Give each person an "Action Covenant." Ask individuals to decide what may be a scapegoat for them. Challenge them to begin to change by fulfilling this covenant.

■ Go

Give each person a 3×5 card. Say: **On this card write a sin you need to turn over to God for forgiveness. Fold the card and use a thumbtack to attach it to the cross. Then sit in silence around the cross.**

Read aloud John 1:29. Then offer this closing prayer: **God, thank you for your son, Jesus, whose sacrifice has given each of us the opportunity for forgiveness. Give us the faith to rely on your promises and accept your gift. In Jesus' name, amen.**

Action Covenant

One scapegoat I use in my life is . . .

One thing I'll do to eliminate using this scapegoat is . . .

Signed . . . .
Witness . . . .
Date . . . .

The 40-Year Goof

■ Theme: Making mistakes (Numbers 1—14)

The book of Numbers contains much more than a simple numbering of the Hebrew people. The book displays both God's protecting hand and his punishing wrath.

The book of Numbers is packed with good and bad news. The Israelites seemed to get their lives in order, only to see their efforts sidetracked by jealousy, complaining and mistakes.

Mistakes haunt teenagers. Young people need to know that God is with them in times of distress, even when they must face the consequences of their blunders. This session centers on God's faithfulness to us even when we take our eyes off him.

■ Objectives

During this session participants will:
● explore Numbers 1—14;
● discuss fair punishment for mistakes young people make;
● discuss Israel's blunders;
● identify how their lives contain mistakes similar to those Israel made; and
● covenant to improve recurring blunders in their lives.

■ Preparation

Read and study Numbers 1—14. Concentrate on chapters 11—14.

Gather newsprint, markers, Bibles and pencils. Make a copy of the "My Blunders" handout and "Action Covenant" for each person.

The Session

■ Dig

Form groups of three, and have groups meet in different parts of the room. Say: **In your group, decide on a fair punishment for each situation I read. You'll have only two minutes to decide.**

After you read each situation, ask a representative from each group to report the punishment chosen. Discuss the groups' ideas.

Situations

1. You broke your curfew by one hour and didn't bother to call to say you'd be late.

2. You forgot to fill the car with gas after using it for a date.

3. Your boyfriend/girlfriend just discovered you've been dating someone else.

4. Your teacher caught you cheating on an exam.

5. At lunch, you ignored a friend because of the group you were eating with.

■ Discover

Say: **It's not easy to decide on fair punishment for mistakes, is it? All of us have different opinions. Israel had to face the harsh reality of what God would do when people consistently went against his will. Let's look at Israel's mistakes as the people headed for the Promised Land.**

Form four groups (a group may be as small as one). Give each group newsprint, markers and a Bible. Assign each group two of the following:

- Complaining, Numbers 11:1-6
- Gluttony, Numbers 11:31-35
- Jealousy, Numbers 12:1-8
- Isolation, Numbers 12:9-16
- Cowardice, Numbers 13:25-33
- Pleading, Numbers 14:13-19
- Judgment, Numbers 14:20-38
- Defeat, Numbers 14:39-45

Say: **After the people fled from Egypt and lived in the Des-**

ert of Sinai, God instructed Moses to appoint leaders from each tribe to take a census of the people. God also told Moses to place the Levites in charge of the tabernacle and to ceremonially purify them.

After the people dedicated the tabernacle, God came down on it in the form of a cloud. Whenever the cloud covered the tabernacle, the people pitched their tents around it. But when the cloud lifted, the Israelites sounded their trumpets and followed the cloud, camping wherever it settled. That's how God led Israel to the Promised Land.

Each of your scripture passages describes a rough time in Israel's history. Read each passage and draw symbolic pictures on your newsprint of what's happening. For example, for jealousy your group might draw two people whispering behind someone's back—like Miriam and Aaron did against Moses. For gluttony your group might draw a table piled high with food.

After groups have finished their pictures, have a volunteer from each group explain the group's symbols. Say: **Israel made a mistake by not believing in God's power to give them the land of Canaan. This time Israel's disobedience brought a severe consequence. God banished the Hebrews to the wilderness for 40 years.**

■ Experience

Give each person a pencil and the "My Blunders" handout. Have kids complete the handout individually. Tape a sheet of newsprint on the wall while group members work. When kids are finished, go over each statement and ask for individual responses to the open-ended statements on the handout. List comments on the newsprint.

Have group members each select one of the themes from the "My Blunders" handout: jealousy, cowardice, mistakes, defeat, gluttony, pleading, complaining or isolation. Have kids each demonstrate a silent sculpture of their theme, and have other group members guess what it is. For example, a person might depict defeat by standing with a look of despair and with his or her head and shoulders slumped forward.

After all have demonstrated their silent sculptures, ask:

What might happen if we consistently refuse to learn from our mistakes?

■ Grow

Reflect again on what happened to the Israelites. Point out Moses' continual effort to save the people from God's wrath. Then ask:

● **Why was God so tough on Miriam and Aaron? on Israel's gluttony? on Israel's cowardice?**

● **What quality did Joshua and Caleb have that the others didn't? How did God respond to Joshua and Caleb?**

● **Was God's final punishment on Israel fair?**

● **In what ways does God discipline you? How is God's discipline now similar to or different from what happened to Israel?**

■ Covenant

Give kids each an "Action Covenant," and have them fill it out. Ask kids each to talk with a partner about one behavior they want to change. Encourage partners to discuss how their lives would change if they eliminated a particular blunder.

■ Go

Say: **Moses intervened to save Israel. How does Jesus intervene for you as your Savior?**

After everyone has responded, close with this prayer: **God, it's hard for us to understand sometimes why we mess up so much. Help us grow in our faith and lean on Jesus as our source of power so we won't be tempted to take our eyes off you. Fill us with your Holy Spirit to lead and empower us. In Jesus' name, amen.**

My Blunders

Instructions: Complete each of the following statements by reflecting on a time when each of these blunders was evident in your life.

I felt defeated
when . . .

I felt isolated
from God when . . .

I became
jealous when . . .

I learned what
it's like to plead for
something when . . .

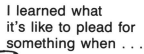

I experienced
judgment for a mistake
I made when . . .

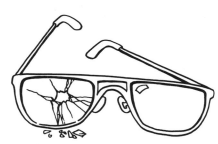

I felt like a
coward when . . .

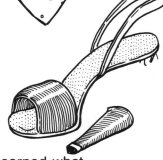

I learned what
happens if I complain
when . . .

I experienced
gluttony when . . .

Action Covenant

One mistake I continue to make is . . .

Something that might help me break the sin cycle in that area is . . .

One person who might help me correct this mistake is . . .

This week I'll work hard on eliminating this mistake from my life by . . .

Signed . . . .
Witness . . . .
Date . . . .

Israel, Meet God!

■ Theme: Knowing and loving God (Deuteronomy 1—11)

Moses' life was nearing its end. The people of Israel had learned much through their wilderness experience. New faces replaced the generation of faithless Hebrews who once stood on the Promised Land's border but were afraid to enter. Now the nation was finally ready for its inheritance.

Moses knew this generation needed to be reminded of what God had done for them. He wanted to motivate the people, so he patiently took the people back through their history, focusing on important events and God's involvement in their lives. This was one of the greatest pep talks ever given about knowing and loving God.

Teenagers often ask questions such as "Who is God?" or "What meaning does God have for my life?" This session enables kids to know God better and find ways they can demonstrate their love for him.

■ Objectives

During this session participants will:
- review Moses' farewell address in Deuteronomy 1—11;
- work together to prepare short speeches that convey what Moses was trying to tell the people about God;
- identify times when God has been with them; and
- discover one way they can love God more.

■ Preparation

Read and study Deuteronomy 1—11.

Gather paper, pencils, Bibles, newsprint and markers. If desired, use a rap music recording (preferably instruments only), and something to play it on. Also bring five sheets, five old extra-large T-shirts and assorted articles of clothing so groups each can design an Old Testament outfit for their Moses character. You'll also need a long table.

Make an "Action Covenant" on a sheet of newsprint. Below the title, write "One thing I will do to begin showing more love for God is . . ." Have it ready to tape on the wall during the Covenant section.

You will also need one copy of the "God Was With Me When . . ." handout for each person.

The Session

■ Dig

Form teams of three to five. Distribute paper and pencils to each team. Tell each team: **You're now a rap group. Create and lead a rap that you think will motivate people to know God better. For example, your group might create something like this** (begin playing the rap music in the background if you have it):

We're here to tell you we've got the word,
Don't be an imbecile, don't be a nerd.
The Lord has spoken, so heed it well,
If you want to know life, then hear what I tell.
Don't boast in your money, don't boast in your fame,
Don't boast in your wisdom (Now that's pretty lame).
But if you've gotta boast, then boast in this:
Say "I know God!" and you'll never miss!

If you don't want to do the sample rap yourself, then have a few kids learn it and do it instead.

When they're ready, have teams take turns presenting their rap songs. Then ask:

● **What does "knowing God" mean to you?**
● **How did your group's rap song motivate people to know God better?**

■ Discover

Say: **The Israelites completed their 40 years of probation in the desert. They had learned much about their God, and this new generation was finally ready to inherit the land. Moses wanted the people to understand God's part in their history, so he retold the nation's story all the way back to Abraham. Today we'll look at what Moses said and why he wanted Israel to remember God's work in the past.**

Form five groups. (A group may be as small as two.) If your group is smaller than 10, use fewer groups and delete one or more of the passages. Give one of the following assignments to each group:

● Deuteronomy 1:1-40
● Deuteronomy 4:1-40
● Deuteronomy 5:1-21
● Deuteronomy 9:1-29
● Deuteronomy 11:1-32

Say: **Work together in your group to write a short speech containing the essence of what Moses was saying.**

■ Experience

After groups each have written their speeches, say: **Select two people in your group to be a Moses character. One person will be Moses' face and feet. The other will be his hands. The rest of your group will design a costume for the Moses character while the two Moses-character people practice the group's speech.**

Select a volunteer and demonstrate the Moses character using this diagram and description:

To create the Moses characters, have groups each choose one person to don an extra-large T-shirt over his or her clothes. Have that person keep both arms straight at his or her sides inside the shirt. Instruct the T-shirted people each to take their shoes off and place them on a table in front of them. Have them each place one hand in each shoe. Then have groups each select another person to thrust his or her arms up into the T-shirt from behind and out through the T-shirt sleeves. Have groups each throw a sheet over the person in back to reduce the distraction. The back person's arms will act as Moses' arms and the front person will act as Moses' face and legs.

Have group members dress their characters and then meet together to listen to all the speeches. Have Moses characters speak in chapter order.

■ Grow

Say: **Moses tried hard to get this new generation to understand that a faithful response to God would always keep the people out of trouble.**

Give each person a "God Was With Me When . . ." handout. Have kids each complete the open-ended statements. Then have kids meet in groups of four and talk about these statements.

After the group discussions, bring the kids together. Then ask:

● **Why is it important to realize when God has been with you?**

● **When you looked back, what did you learn about God's presence in your life?**

● **Why did Moses want to remind Israel about God's presence in their lives before they entered Canaan?**

● **In what way is God at work in your life?**

● **How do you know that the God who's with you is the same God that was with the Israelites during Moses' time?**

■ Covenant

Read aloud Deuteronomy 6:4-5. Ask:

● **What does it mean to love God with your entire being?**

● **What are ways you feel you might not be loving God?**

Tape the "Action Covenant" you created on the wall. Give kids markers and have them write on the newsprint how they can love God more. Have everyone sign and date the "Action Covenant" newsprint.

■ Go

Read aloud 1 John 5:3-5. Ask kids to share why they wrote what they did. Ask kids to pray for each other during the week. Close with prayer.

God Was With Me When . . .

Instructions: Think about those moments when you realized God was with you. Complete each open-ended statement with a brief description of an experience that illustrates when you knew God was there.

God was with me during a crisis when . . .

God was with me during a time of peer pressure when . . .

God was with me in my family when . . .

God was with me in a friendship when . . .

God was with me in a big decision when . . .

Taking the Promised Land

■ Theme: Fighting battles (Joshua 6—11)

Canaan contained several city-states, each with great walls protecting its inhabitants. Although each city functioned as a separate kingdom with its own king, the people of different cities would sometimes join forces against a common threat. The Hebrews presented just such a threat to the people of Canaan. And the Canaanites weren't about to let them take their land without a fight.

Teenagers experience numerous battles—with peer pressure, identity, family problems, friendships, teachers—and the list continues to grow. This session focuses on battles and how to win them.

■ Objectives

During this session participants will:

● explore the conquest of Canaan as recorded in Joshua 6—11;

● go through simulation activities to develop a strategy for working together; and

● identify the battles currently affecting their lives.

■ Preparation

Read and study Joshua 6—11.

Gather Bibles, pencils, paper, newsprint, markers and masking tape. Get two reams of paper, each a different color.

Purchase or borrow the song "Giants in the Land" on the album *Giants in the Land* (Word), recorded by Wayne Watson. You'll also need equipment to play it on. If you can't obtain this album, find a recording of another song about God's help in times of struggle.

Make one copy of the "Battle Zones" handout for each person.

The Session

■ Dig

Tell group members they're going to participate in a simulation experience involving strategy. Designate a place in the middle of the room to be a river. Form groups of eight or more and read aloud the following directions. If you have fewer than eight people, use one of each character instead of two.

Farmer's Riddle

1. Appoint group members to play the following eight roles: two chickens, two foxes, two bags of grain and two farmers. Each person must take on the characteristics of his or her new identity. For example, the chickens can only cluck and the bags of grain can only lie around until the farmers move them.

2. The farmers must physically carry the chickens, foxes and bags of grain across the river. And the farmers must always travel together.

3. The foxes can't be left unsupervised with the chickens or they'll eat them; the chickens can't be left unattended with the grain or they'll eat it. Challenge each group to get across the river.*

Farmer's Riddle Solution

Draw from the following solution to create hints for your group if they have trouble solving the riddle:

1. The farmers carry the chickens across the river, leaving the foxes and the grain.

2. The farmers return and then carry the foxes (or the grain) across.

3. On their return trip, the farmers carry the chickens *back* to the first side of the river.

4. The farmers then take the grain (or the foxes) across, leaving the chickens.

5. The farmers return and carry the chickens across.

After groups have struggled with this problem for a while, ask:
● **Did you accomplish the goal?**
● **What kind of strategy did your group develop to accomplish the goal?**
● **What was easy about the decisions your group needed to make? What was difficult?**

*This "Farmer's Riddle" activity was taken from *Building Community in Youth Groups*, (Group Books, by Denny Rydberg). Used by permission.

■ Discover

Say: **Let's explore Joshua 6—11. We'll see why a military strategy was important to the Israelites if they were going to overcome Canaan.**

Canaan was full of walled cities, each city with its own king. We'll see how Joshua, a great strategist, was able to win battle after battle because he let God lead him.

Form six groups (a group may be one person). Hand each group Bibles, pencils, paper, newsprint and markers. Give each group one of the following assignments:

- Joshua 6
- Joshua 7
- Joshua 8
- Joshua 9
- Joshua 10
- Joshua 11:1-15

Say: **Read your assigned scripture. Then write a military-style briefing based on what took place. Stick with the facts and only a few details. Prepare a report for the total group as if you are a military panel reviewing the events. Decide who in your group will be your commander, and then let him or her describe what happened. For example, the commander for the battle at Jericho might say, "The weapons for this seven-day struggle were powerful trumpets—that's right, only trumpets. Each day we . . ." Then he or she would briefly describe the battle and the strategy behind it.**

After all commanders have presented their briefings, ask:
- **What did you learn from these reports?**
- **Why did God want Israel to destroy all the people?**
- **If Joshua hadn't totally destroyed the cultures that worshiped idols, what might have happened to the Israelites later on?**
- **How do you feel about this type of destruction?**

■ Experience

Form two teams. Put a strip of masking tape on the floor to divide the room. Place teams on opposite sides of the tape and give teams equal stacks of paper. One team should have one color, and the other team should have the other color. Say: **On "go," wad up each sheet of paper and throw it across the line at the other team. On "stop," the team with the most paper on the other side wins. There are only two rules: You can't cross the line into the other team's territory at any time, and you must wad each piece of paper individually before throwing it. Take time to develop your strategy. I'll give you a 10-second warning before you are to begin.**

Allow two minutes for teams to develop their strategies. Give a 10-second warning, say "Go" and allow for a two-minute battle. Once you say "Stop," count the wads of paper by color and see who wins.

Have kids meet together and debrief. Ask:
- **What kind of strategy did you use?**
- **Did the other team cheat? How?**
- **Why did you put so much energy into throwing wads of paper at the other team?**
- **Is it fun to battle other people at times? Why or why not?**

Give each person a "Battle Zones" handout. Have kids each complete the open-ended statements, then discuss their responses as a total group.

■ Grow

After the discussion, ask:
- **Do you ever get tired of fighting battles? Why or why not?**
- **How do you decide if something is worth fighting for?**
- **What's one battle you're fighting that you feel you must win?**
- **What battle is Jesus fighting to help you win?**
- **What role does God play in our battles?**

■ Go

Say: **Throughout history people have been fighting battles. Jesus came to finish the war Satan wages for our souls. Paul says, "In all these things we are more than conquerors through him who loved us. For I am convinced that neither death nor life, neither angels nor demons, neither the present nor the future, nor any powers, neither height nor depth, nor anything else in all creation, will be able to separate us from the love of God that is in Christ Jesus our Lord" (Romans 8:37-39).**

Ask:

What do these verses mean?

After a brief discussion, encourage kids to think about the battles they face. Play the song "Giants in the Land" by Wayne Watson. Close with prayer.

Battle Zones

Instructions: Like the Israelites, we always seem to be fighting some kind of battle. What battles are you fighting? Write your response to each statement below.

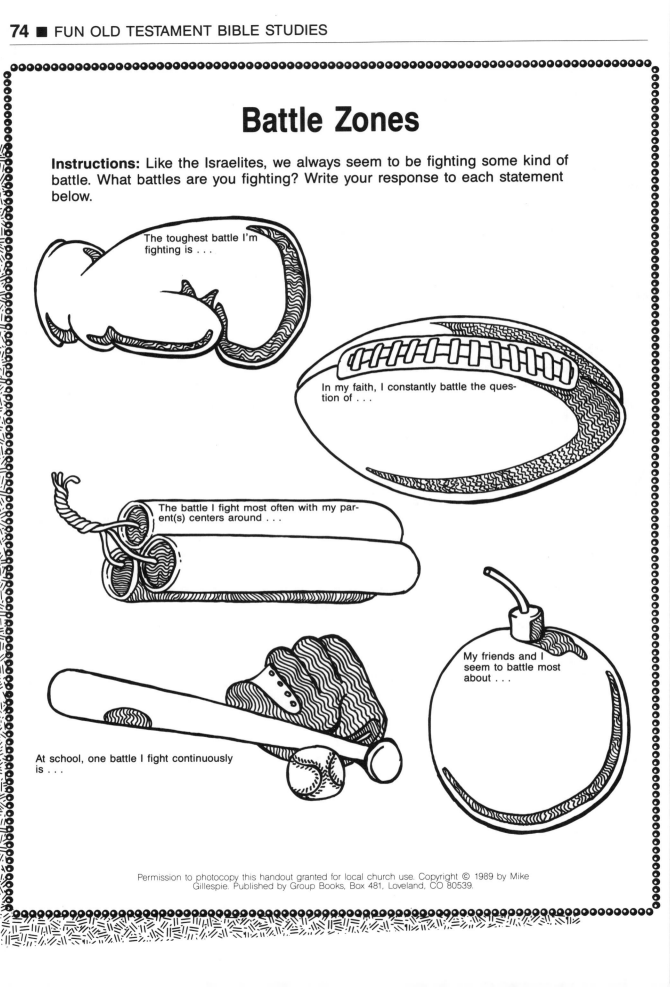

The toughest battle I'm fighting is . . .

In my faith, I constantly battle the question of . . .

The battle I fight most often with my parent(s) centers around . . .

My friends and I seem to battle most about . . .

At school, one battle I fight continuously is . . .

Who Will You Serve?

■ Theme: Living in God's promises (Joshua 12—24)

Joshua's faith shined brightly. He knew God had given Canaan to the Israelites. And like Moses, Joshua wanted the people to understand what had happened. So he reminded the people God had kept his promise to give them a homeland. Then he challenged them to continue in their faithfulness to God.

Promises bring hope. In a time when teenagers face countless broken promises—from friends, parents, society, even themselves—they need to know they can trust God's promises. This session focuses on God's faithfulness. It helps young people find hope in kept promises.

■ Objectives

During this session participants will:
● explore Joshua 12—24;
● discuss the importance of keeping promises;
● learn about Canaan's division among the 12 tribes;
● discuss the importance of Joshua's farewell address;
● make predictions about each other's future; and
● covenant to keep a promise.

■ Preparation

Read and study Joshua 12—24.

Gather 3×5 cards, newsprint, markers, Bibles, pencils and masking tape. Make a copy of the "Friendship Predictions" handout and the "Action Covenant" for each person.

The Session

■ Dig

Hand each person a 3×5 card. Ask kids each to complete this statement on their card (tell kids their cards will be read aloud):

"I remember _____ kept his or her promise of_____

_____."

when _____

For example, one person might say, "I remember our teacher kept his promise of no homework for a week when our math class made all A's and B's on our midterm test."

When group members have completed their statements, collect the cards. Read the cards aloud one at a time. Be careful not to identify the card's author in front of the group (to avoid embarrassing anyone).

Then ask:

● **Why are promises important?**
● **How do you feel when people break promises?**

After a few people respond, say: **Unlike people, God has never broken a promise. Let's look at the book of Joshua's last chapters and see how God kept his promises to Israel.**

■ Discover

Give a brief summary of Joshua 12—22, then say: **Imagine God had prepared a beautiful land somewhere on Earth. And he came and offered it to you, saying: "I have set this land apart just for you. It's yours. I'm not giving it to you because you deserve it or because of anything you've done. I'm giving it to you just because I love you."**

Ask:

How would that make you feel?

Form two groups and give each group newsprint, markers and Bibles. Assign chapter 23 to one group and chapter 24 to the other. Ask groups each to read their chapter and decide on the five most important points Joshua was trying to make. Have groups list these points on newsprint and report them to the total group.

After both groups have reported, ask:

● **If you had been there, how would you have responded to Joshua's speech?**
● **Why did Joshua stress the points that he did?**

■ Experience

Give each person a pencil, masking tape and the "Friendship Predictions" handout. Say: **Have a friend tape your handout to** your back. **The people in this room are going to predict your future based on the promises in God's Word and the abilities they see God has given you. Think seriously about what you will write on another person's sheet. Only two rules apply: Everything you write must be encouraging, and don't make jokes.**

Allow kids to complete the statements on each other's sheets. Remind kids that they're writing predictions for the other people in the room and not for themselves. After about 10 minutes, go around and make sure everyone has something written under each statement. Encourage kids to finish any uncompleted handouts. When everyone is done, have kids each look at their sheet.

■ Grow

Then ask:

● **What was most important for you to write on people's sheets?**

● **How is this similar to what Joshua needed to say to Israel?**

● **How did Joshua try to challenge his peers?**

● **How did you try to challenge your peers?**

● **What danger were those foreign gods for Israel? What danger do misguided ideas have for you?**

● **Why must we recognize what God has done and continues to do in our lives?**

● **What promises has God made to you?**

● **Why do you think some promises aren't fulfilled right away?**

■ Covenant

Give each person an "Action Covenant." Ask kids each to pair up and complete their covenant. Read aloud John 10:10 and have each pair discuss:

● **What does the promise of abundant life mean to you?**

● **How can abundant life happen for you?**

● **How can you help the promise of abundant life come true for others?**

■ Go

Gather everyone in a circle and read aloud Joshua 24:14-15. Ask kids each to complete this prayer, "God, help me keep my promise to serve you by . . ." For example, one person might say "by being faithful in a daily prayer time and scripture reading." After everyone has offered his or her prayer, close with hugs.

Friendship Predictions

One decision I'll need to make soon is . . .

The greatest challenge I face is . . .

The greatest opportunity awaiting me is . . .

One special ability God has given me is . . .

If I ignore God's grace in my life, I may never . . .

God has prepared me for my future by . . .

One promise God has given me is . . .

Action Covenant

One promise I've made, but failed to keep is . . .

To correct this mistake, this week I'll . . .

Signed . . . .
Witness . . . .
Date . . . .

The Hebrew Roller Coaster

■ Theme: Facing life's changes (Judges 1—10)

The book of Judges describes the Hebrews' roller-coaster ride through prosperity and adversity. Israel forgot to obey God and began to worship Canaan's gods, so God allowed Israel to fall into the hands of foreign conquerors. The people then cried for God to save them, so God sent a judge to rescue them. The people responded in faithful obedience for a time, but then the cycle repeated itself again and again.

Teenagers bounce back and forth between good and bad times. Their daily lives reflect this constant struggle. This session offers kids hope in the good and bad times they experience.

■ Objectives

During this session participants will:
- explore Judges 1—10;
- identify moments of prosperity and adversity in their lives;
- discuss a judge's role in Israel;
- present a drama of Gideon's life as Israel's judge; and
- explore the adversity Christ suffered on their behalf.

■ Preparation

Read and study Judges 1—10.

Gather pencils, paper, Bibles, newsprint and markers. Make a copy of the "Good Times/Bad Times" and "Gideon—A Play in Three Acts" handouts for each person.

Secure the following props for the play: a robe for Gideon, a shaggy rug for a fleece, a halo for the angel, a rope, a toy trumpet, an empty jar and a king's crown. Set up a stage area.

The Session

■ Dig

Give each person a pencil and a "Good Times/Bad Times" handout. Say: **This profile traces the past 10 months of your life. Follow the instructions on the handout.**

Have kids share and discuss their profiles. Ask:

● **What have the past 10 months been like for you—a time of adversity or prosperity? Why?**

● **What got you through times of adversity?**

● **How did you deal with times of prosperity?**

● **Were any of these times significant in your relationship with your friends? your family? God? Explain.**

■ Discover

Form two groups, and give each person paper and a Bible. Say: **The book of Judges explores the Hebrews' struggle with prosperity and adversity. The people bounced back and forth between the two extremes. They caused many of their own problems because they kept turning to Canaan's idols.**

Ask one group to read Judges 2:6-23 and prepare to report on the following questions:

● **Who were the judges?**

● **Why do you think God was angry with the Israelites?**

Have the other group skim Judges 3—4 and prepare to report on the following questions:

● **How did the judges bring peace to Israel?**

● **Why did God continue to deliver Israel even though the people consistently rebelled against him?**

Have each group report its findings to the other group.

■ Experience

After both groups have reported, say: **One of the most interesting judges was Gideon. We'll explore his story by creating a three-act play.**

Distribute the "Gideon—A Play in Three Acts" handout. Form three groups and assign each group one act. Have at least one person be narrator to read the opening scripture and introduce each scene. Have groups read their scripture passages and prepare creative presentations of their material. Encourage kids to use their imaginations without changing the facts. Let kids know they can use props to aid their character portrayals.

When all groups are ready, have the narrator introduce each act.

After the play, ask:

● **What similarities do you see between yourself and Gideon?**

● **How do you and Gideon differ?**

● **Was Gideon stupid to go into battle with such odds against him? Why or why not?**

● **In what ways was God at work in Gideon's life?**

● **What conclusions can we draw from Gideon's life about God's work in our lives?**

■ Grow

Say: **Think back to your "Good Times/Bad Times" handout. Compare your good and bad times with the Israelites' good and bad times.**

Ask:

● **Why did the Hebrews prosper during the time a judge was alive?**

● **Should Christians expect all good times simply because they believe in God? Why or why not?**

● **Gideon went into battle against impossible odds. When have you faced seemingly impossible odds? How did your faith help?**

● **Look again at your profile. How many months of adversity did you cause? Why?**

■ Go

Tape newsprint on the wall. Say: **Think about Jesus' life. Let's list Jesus' moments of prosperity and adversity.**

When kids have run out of suggestions, have a volunteer read Matthew 26:63-68. Say: **Jesus endured adversity so we could share in God's prosperity.**

Form a circle and ask:

What adversities are you facing that you'd like the group to pray about?

After individuals have responded, ask specific group members to pray for these people during the week.

Close with the following prayer: **God, thank you for the sacrifice of your Son so that our adversity can be turned into prosperity. Help us live lives worthy of that supreme sacrifice. Use our failures to teach us how to serve you in faith. In Jesus' name, amen.**

Good Times/Bad Times

Instructions: On the center line, write in the last 10 months from right to left—beginning with the current month. For example, if this is June, write "June" after the A, "May" after the B, and so on. Then rate each month from +5 for good times to −5 for bad times. Connect the numbers—from the left to the right—to show your Prosperity/Adversity profile for the past 10 months.

G O O D   T I M E S

+5 _____

+4 _____

+3 _____

+2 _____

+1 _____

J_____I_____H_____G_____F_____E_____D_____C_____B_____A_____

−1 _____

−2 _____

−3 _____

−4 _____

−5 _____

B A D   T I M E S

Note why you rated each month as you did.

A _____

B _____

C _____

D _____

E _____

F _____

G _____

H _____

I _____

J _____

Gideon—A Play in Three Acts

Introduction (Judges 6:1-10)

ACT 1   Scene 1—Gideon's call (Judges 6:11-24)

Scene 2—Gideon destroys Baal (Judges 6:25-35)

Scene 3—Gideon's fleece (Judges 6:36-40)

ACT 2   Scene 1—Selecting the 300 men (Judges 7:1-8)

Scene 2—Prophecy and battle orders (Judges 7:9-18)

Scene 3—The battle (Judges 7:19-25)

ACT 3   Scene 1—Trouble with Ephraim (Judges 8:1-3)

Scene 2—Dealing with Succoth and Peniel (Judges 8:4-9, 13-17)

Scene 3—Zebah and Zalmunna (Judges 8:10-12, 19-21)

Scene 4—Gideon refuses kingship (Judges 8:22-28)

Stand By Me

■ Theme: Being loyal (Ruth)

The book of Ruth presents a drama without heroic acts or spectacular scenes. But the central characters, Ruth, Naomi and Boaz, demonstrated strong convictions and faith.

Ruth's loyalty to her mother-in-law provided Ruth—a foreigner—an opportunity to marry Boaz and enter the Hebrew community. She became an ancestress to King David.

This session helps young people understand the importance of loyalty in relationships with people and with God.

■ Objectives

During this session participants will:
- explore the book of Ruth;
- discuss what loyalty means in their lives; and
- examine the loyalty characteristics they see in those around them.

■ Preparation

Read and study the book of Ruth. Read the Hebrew law in Deuteronomy 25:5-10.

Gather markers, newsprint, masking tape, Bibles and pencils. Make a copy of the "Person of the Year" entry form for each person.

Write each of the following headings on a separate sheet of newsprint:
- In a friendship, loyalty means . . .
- In a family, loyalty means . . .
- In a relationship with God, loyalty means . . .

The Session

■ Dig

Form three groups. Give each group a marker and one of the newsprint sheets you prepared. Say: **Loyalty is an important part of life. Your group has been assigned one particular area in which loyalty is important. List five ways loyalty shows up in this area. Be specific. For example, in friendship, loyalty means not talking behind a friend's back.**

After groups are finished, tape their lists on the wall and talk about each group's ideas.

Then ask:

Without loyalty, how would life be different?

■ Discover

After a brief discussion, form four groups. Give each group newsprint and markers, and give each person a Bible. Assign each group a chapter of Ruth and say: **Today we're going to explore the book of Ruth. This story takes place during the period of the Judges. Read the chapter assigned to your group and pick out the positive qualities you see in Ruth. List them on your newsprint. For example, your list might contain statements such as:**

● **Ruth was loyal, faithful, persevering and loving; or**

● **Ruth showed she was a hard worker by gathering food from Boaz's fields and helping her mother-in-law.**

After groups complete their lists, tape the lists on the wall. Then ask:

● **What was your impression of Ruth? Naomi? Boaz? Why?**

● **What loyalties were most important to Ruth?**

● **Which of Ruth's loyal qualities are important to you?**

● **Why do you think the book of Ruth was included in the Bible?**

■ Experience

Say: **At first glance we might not recognize Ruth's special traits. She had a gentle spirit and didn't talk a lot about herself. She simply shared her faith in a quiet, loyal way.**

Often the people around us go unnoticed like Ruth did. Sometimes we neglect our sense of loyalty toward the people who mean the most to us.

Form two groups. Give each person a pencil and a "Person of the Year" entry form. Say: **Work together in your group to nominate each person in the other group as "Person of the Year."**

Have groups complete their forms. Then bring the groups together and ask a volunteer from each group to read the nominations from his or her group.

Ask:

● **How do you feel about making these recommendations? Why?**

● **How does it feel to be recommended? Why?**

■ Grow

Say: **Many times we feel we don't have much to offer. We see beautiful, gifted people receiving recognition while we go unnoticed. We may sometimes feel that our loyalty to family, friends and God isn't worth much.**

Ask:

● **Who or what are you most loyal to?**

● **What does loyalty have to do with character and self-worth?**

● **When have you experienced broken loyalty in a friendship? in your family? in your relationship with God?**

● **How do you feel when someone is disloyal to you?**

● **How has God been loyal to you?**

■ Go

Have volunteers read aloud John 15:13 and Romans 5:8. Ask kids each to name someone they feel exemplifies loyalty. Then close with this prayer: **God, when we study Ruth we realize how important loyalty is. Help us grow in loyalty to others. In Jesus' name, amen.**

Person of the Year

Entry Form

TO: The National Awards Committee

RE: Entry form for _____, our Person of the Year

    We hereby recommend the above-named person for Person of the Year. We recommend this individual for the following reasons:

1. _____ possesses the following positive characteristics:

      A. _____

      B. _____

      C. _____

      D. _____

2. _____ demonstrates uniqueness through:

_____

_____

3. _____ demonstrates faith in God by:

_____

_____

4. _____ will go far in life because:

_____

_____

We highly recommend _____ because he or she has blessed others by:

How Far Should a Friendship Go?

■ Theme: Staying faithful to friends (1 Samuel 16—20)

These chapters in 1 Samuel detail one of the most powerful friendships described in the Old Testament. David became best friends with Jonathan, King Saul's son. The two young men modeled a friendship that provides important insights for relationships.

This session helps young people explore friendship and courage and discover how to be more faithful to their friends.

■ Objectives

During this session participants will:
- explore 1 Samuel 16—20;
- discuss David's courage;
- focus on the friendship between David and Jonathan;
- identify specific, important friendship qualities; and
- covenant to strengthen a current friendship.

■ Preparation

Read and study 1 Samuel 16—20.

Gather markers, masking tape, newsprint, Bibles, pencils, construction paper, the song "Friends" by Michael W. Smith and a stereo. If you can't obtain this song, use another song about friendships.

Make a copy of the "Action Covenant" for each person. Make five copies of the "My Perfect Friend" handout.

Cut the construction paper into 2×2-inch pieces so each person has 10 pieces. Write "A friend is a person who . . ." on newsprint and tape it on the wall.

Also prepare five stacks of 15 same-color 2×2-inch pieces of construction paper.

Tape a long sheet of newsprint lengthwise across one wall of the room (several shorter sheets will also work). Across the top, space evenly the words "Heart," "Courage," "Jealousy," "Friendship," "Hatred" and "Oaths."

The Session

■ Dig

Give each person a marker and 10 2×2-inch pieces of paper. Have individuals write on their 2×2-inch pieces of paper as many responses as they can think of to the statement "A friend is a person who . . ." Ask kids to write only one response on each piece of paper. A person might write, "makes me laugh" or "never puts me down."

As individuals finish, have them tape their paper pieces anywhere on the newsprint with "A friend is a person who . . ." written on it. After kids have hung their paper pieces, read the responses aloud to the group.

Then ask:

How have your friendships changed your life?

■ Discover

After a brief discussion, say: **Although Saul started out as a good king, he wasn't a good king in his later years. Following God's instructions, Samuel anointed David, the shepherd boy, as Saul's successor. Two of the first stories we read about David involve his experience with Goliath, the giant Philistine, and his relationship with Jonathan, Saul's son. Let's learn more about David's courage and his friendship with Jonathan.**

Form five teams (a team can be one person). Give each team a stack of 15 same-color 2×2-inch pieces of paper, and give each person a Bible and pencil. Assign each team one of the chapters in 1 Samuel 16—20. Tell team members to skim their chapters and find examples of the six topics listed on the newsprint—Heart, Courage, Jealousy, Friendship, Hatred and Oaths.

Have team members each write on one 2×2-inch piece of paper a scripture verse or series of verses that applies to one of the six topics and explain why. For example, one person might list 1 Samuel 16:7 on the card and write, "God looked upon David's heart to see his value." Another person might list 1 Samuel 17:45-46 and write, "This scripture describes David's courage when he approached the Philistine giant." Challenge teams to see which one can fill up the most cards and tape them on the newsprint in the proper area. Limit the activity to five to 10 minutes.

Bring your whole group together. Ask volunteers to read the 2×2-inch pieces of paper in each category. After all the papers are read, ask:

● **What does it mean that God looks at the heart and not at physical features?**

● **Where did David get his courage? Does the source of his courage have any significance to you? Why or why not?**

● **Jonathan and David "became one in spirit" (1 Samuel 18:1). What does that mean? Could you use that phrase to describe your friendships? Why or why not?**

● **How do Saul's actions illustrate what happens when hatred enters a person's life?**

■ Experience

Have people return to their groups. Give each group a long sheet of newsprint, a marker and the "My Perfect Friend" handout. Say: **We know how important friends are. We also know how terrible we can feel when we think our friends have deserted us.**

Your group is going to create the perfect friend. On your sheet of newsprint trace around one group member's body, and label the top of the page "My Perfect Friend." Then follow the instructions on the "My Perfect Friend" handout.

After groups are finished, have everyone meet together and tape the body outlines on the wall. Discuss a perfect friend's characteristics. Ask:

● **Which of these friendship characteristics do your friends possess? Give an example.**

● **What is your strongest friendship characteristic? How do you know?**

■ Grow

Say: **God wants us to develop wholesome friendships. David and Jonathan's friendship was so powerful because it was based on mutual love and respect.**

Ask:

● **How would David's life have been different without Jonathan's friendship? Explain.**

Play the song "Friends" by Michael W. Smith. Then ask:

● **How does God work through our friendships?**

● **What happens when we expect friends to be perfect? Is that ever possible? Why or why not?**

● **What's the best gift you could give your friend? What's the best gift he or she could give you? Explain your answers.**

● **What's the greatest risk you've ever taken for a friend? What's the greatest risk a friend's ever taken for you? How do you feel about these experiences?**

■ Covenant

Give each person an "Action Covenant." Have kids each complete their covenant and agree to share it with a friend. Encourage group members to support one another during the week by reminding each other of this assignment.

■ Go

Place a chair in the center of the room and ask group members to form a circle around that chair. Have group members take turns sitting in the chair. Have the other group members tell the person in the chair what friendship characteristics they appreciate about him or her. (Note: This activity is powerful. Some young people may hesitate to go through it, but they'll remember the affirmation for a long time once they experience it.)

Close with this prayer: **God, thanks for loving each of us so much. Help us remember to share your love with others. Remind us to see Jonathan and David's friendship as a model for our friendships. Our friends are so important; help us not take them for granted. In Jesus' name, amen.**

My Perfect Friend

Instructions: Read these open-ended statements concerning what a perfect friend would do in the following situations. Work as a team to complete each statement. Write your responses in the appropriate places on your large body outline.

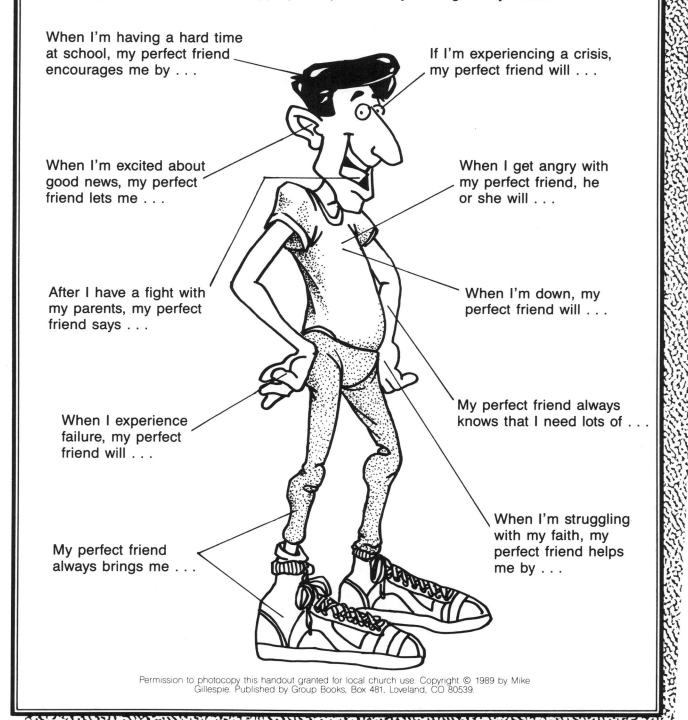

When I'm having a hard time at school, my perfect friend encourages me by . . .

If I'm experiencing a crisis, my perfect friend will . . .

When I'm excited about good news, my perfect friend lets me . . .

When I get angry with my perfect friend, he or she will . . .

After I have a fight with my parents, my perfect friend says . . .

When I'm down, my perfect friend will . . .

When I experience failure, my perfect friend will . . .

My perfect friend always knows that I need lots of . . .

My perfect friend always brings me . . .

When I'm struggling with my faith, my perfect friend helps me by . . .

Action Covenant

The thing I appreciate most about my friend is . . .

The part of our friendship that I tend to take for granted is . . .

The next time I see my friend, I'll express how much he or she means to me by saying . . .

Signed . . . .
Witness . . . .
Date . . . .

Sin? What Sin?

■ Theme: Hiding your sin (2 Samuel 11—12)

Second Samuel 11—12 describes David's struggle with his sinful nature. This great man of God fell prey to the lure of sexual sin. To make matters worse, David tried to disguise his sin.

When teenagers give in to temptation, they sometimes try to cover it up rather than face the consequences of their actions. Like David, they search for the easy way out—even if it involves deceit. This session helps teenagers realize that all of us sin and must learn to accept the consequences of our actions.

■ Objectives

During this session participants will:

- study 2 Samuel 11—12;
- discuss the consequences of their wrong choices;
- present a drama of the events in the scripture passage;
- debate who was responsible for David's sin; and
- confess one sin area they've been covering up.

■ Preparation

Read and study 2 Samuel 11—12.

Gather newsprint, masking tape, markers, Bibles, paper, pencils and a hand-held mirror.

Write each of the following headings on a separate sheet of newsprint and tape the sheets on the wall:

- Taking drugs
- Driving too fast
- Driving while intoxicated
- Having sex before marriage
- Backstabbing a friend
- Running away from home
- Putting down a teacher
- Cheating on a test
- Ignoring your curfew
- Having poor eating habits
- Blaming others for your mistake
- Lying to others

Using the construction paper and string, make signs for kids to hang around their necks. Write one of these names on each sign: David, Bathsheba, Uriah, Joab or Nathan. On two signs write, Messenger/Servant. Gather different kinds of cloth, ribbon and jewelry to use as clothing props.

The Session

■ Dig

Give each person a marker. Say: **Look at the newsprint on the walls. Assume you've committed each of these sins. What possible consequences would you face? On each sheet, write one possible consequence.**

After most people have written on each sheet, have group members meet together. Read the consequences and discuss them. Then ask:

● **When God forgives your sin, does he eliminate the sin's consequences? Explain.**

● **When you get caught doing something wrong, what do you tend to do? Why?**

● **Have you ever made a situation worse by trying to cover up a mistake? Explain.**

■ Discover

Say: **Today we'll be studying the story of David and Bathsheba.**

Give each person a Bible and ask for volunteers to role-play 2 Samuel 11—12.

Enlist volunteers to play these seven characters: David, Bathsheba, Uriah, Joab, Nathan and two servants/messengers. Give the appropriate sign to each character. Have all group members create costumes for the characters from the items you collected. Divide 2 Samuel 11:5—12:23 into several parts and select a narrator for each part. Allow the narrators time to practice.

Once narrators and characters are prepared, say: **I'll read the first four verses to set the stage. Then the narrators will read their parts, pausing for the characters to silently act out what's happening.**

After you've read 2 Samuel 11:1-4, have narrators and characters begin.

After the drama, ask:

● **Why was David so obsessed with covering up his actions?**

● **David already had many wives. Why do you think he was so attracted to Bathsheba?**

● **What makes us want things that aren't ours? Can you think of a time you wanted something that wasn't yours? What happened?**

● **Should rulers or leaders have special privileges? Why or why not?**

■ Experience

Say: **Who was to blame for David's sin? Was it simply lust on David's part, or did Bathsheba lure David into sin? Let's debate.**

Have group members separate into two equal groups. Give each group paper and pencil, and have each group list arguments to support its position. Ask group #1 to prove it was Bathsheba's fault. Ask group #2 to prove it was David's fault. Have each group select three people to argue its position in the debate.

After five to 10 minutes, have the two groups meet together and hold the debate. Have each group give a one-minute opening statement. Then allow orderly interaction for about three minutes. Finally, give each group one minute for closing remarks.

■ Grow

After the debate, ask:

● **Which side won? What good points were made?**

● **Was there anything positive in the story of David and Bathsheba? Explain.**

● **How are you like David?**

● **How are you like Bathsheba?**

● **Why didn't God condemn David and void his covenant with David? How do God's actions toward David relate to you?**

● **In what areas of life do people tend to hide their sin most? Why do they hide such things?**

■ Go

Gather everyone in a circle. Review the confrontation between Nathan and David. Emphasize Nathan's statement, "You are the man!" (2 Samuel 12:7). Have individuals each think of a situation in which God could say that to them.

Pass a hand-held mirror around the group. Ask kids each to share, as they receive the mirror, a cover-up they need to confess and be forgiven for. Allow kids to pass on the mirror silently if they don't wish to share. Watch for kids who choose to pass. Meet with them individually at a later time. See if they need to talk about a problem they felt uncomfortable sharing with the group.

Close with the following prayer: **God, help us use your strength to accept the consequences of our actions. Help us follow David's example in accepting your forgiveness and moving on to live according to your will. In Jesus' name, amen.**

One Against a Nation

■ Theme: Standing up for your beliefs (1 Kings 17—22)

First Kings 17—22 tells the story of the prophet Elijah. This great prophet emerged during the reign of the evil King Ahab and his wicked wife Jezebel. While the people turned from God to worship the Canaanite god, Baal, Elijah became the champion of truth in Israel.

Elijah stood up for God against formidable odds. He challenged more than 450 Baal prophets to a contest and won. But later, he fled from the king's evil wife Jezebel.

This session helps teenagers understand why they are sometimes afraid to take a stand, and challenges them to hold to their beliefs.

■ Objectives

During this session participants will:
- explore 1 Kings 17—22, focusing on Elijah's life;
- discuss the "fight or flight" moments of Elijah's life;
- write a "letter to the editor" about a particular concern; and
- discuss ways they are called to fight or speak out.

■ Preparation

Read and study 1 Kings 17—22.

Gather markers, Bibles and pencils. Tape a 6-foot sheet of newsprint on the wall. Make a copy of the "Letter to the Editor" handout for each person.

Read the editorial pages of various newspapers for a few days. Cut out several letters to the editor on different topics, one for each youth group member.

You'll also need a pitcher of grape juice, an uncut loaf of bread, a paper cup for each person, two free-standing candles, and matches. Note: This is for a communion service. Consult with and follow the direction of your senior minister in conducting this part of the session.

The Session

■ Dig

Give each person a letter to the editor from a newspaper. Have kids each read their letter and identify what the writer is standing up for. Ask group members to share their findings with the group. Then ask:

● **Why do you think a person would write a letter to the editor?**

● **What good might come from this letter?**

● **Do you think only certain kinds of people write these letters? Explain your answer.**

■ Discover

Say: **Today we'll learn about a man who stood up for God even when the whole nation of Israel turned to worship Baal, the god of the Canaanites. God sent his prophet Elijah to show Israel there's only one true God. He gave this prophet the ability to prove that Baal was powerless.**

Form four groups and give each person a marker and a Bible. Assign each group one of these chapters: 1 Kings 17, 18, 19 or 21. Ask each group to read its chapter and illustrate it on the newsprint on the wall. For example, the group that reads chapter 17 might sketch a river and some ravens with food in their beaks.

Bring the groups together and ask each group to explain its drawing. When the groups are finished, add any important details and give background on chapters 20 and 22. Then ask:

● **Why did Elijah destroy all the prophets of Baal after he won the challenge?**

● **Why did Elijah run from Jezebel?**

● **Do you think Elijah was cowardly or smart to run? Why?**

● **When Elijah was in the wilderness, why did he want to die?**

● **What made Elijah willing to face Ahab again?**

■ Experience

Say: **Elijah stood up for what he believed, yet he also struggled when others came against him. Think of an issue you feel strongly about. The issue could be something at your school, in your home, in the community or around the world. You might select an issue such as cheating or abortion. Think about what you would say in a letter to the editor about this issue.**

Give each person a pencil and a "Letter to the Editor" handout.

Have each person complete the form.

After a few minutes, bring kids together and ask them each to read aloud their letter. Then ask:

● **Why do you have such strong feelings about the issue in your letter?**

● **What effect would a letter like yours have?**

● **In what other ways can we stand up for something we believe?**

■ Grow

Say: **Taking a stand is risky. Elijah discovered this when Jezebel threatened to kill him after he destroyed her precious prophets. The risk of standing up for something often keeps us quiet.**

Ask:

● **When have you stood up for what you believed even though others were against you? Explain what happened.**

● **What are consequences you've faced for speaking out against your friends' beliefs? your parents'? your church leaders'? your school teachers' or administrators'?**

● **When did you have strong feelings about something but remained silent? Explain what happened.**

Have a volunteer read aloud Matthew 12:9-14. Have group members suggest other occasions when Jesus said or did something that got him in trouble. Then ask:

● **How do you think Jesus decided whether to confront or withdraw?**

● **How do you decide whether to confront or withdraw?**

● **How is your faith involved in this decision?**

■ Go

Close the session with a communion service. (Remember to discuss this communion service with your senior minister in advance.)

Give each person a paper cup. Place the uncut loaf of bread and a pitcher of grape juice on a table in the center of the room. Light the two free-standing candles and place them on opposite sides of the bread. Dim the lights. Have individuals circle around the communion setting. Say: **All of us are concerned about standing up for our belief in Christ. Each of us must decide daily whether we will be bold about our faith or remain silent.**

When we take communion, we're identifying with Christ's suffering and remembering what he did for us on the cross. We're saying we've given our lives to Christ to use however he desires. We're also saying we're one with each other and are dedicated to supporting each other. By taking communion, we're agreeing to stand out from the crowd and to stand up for

what we believe. You must decide in your heart what you will do.

Without speaking, walk to the center of the circle, pinch off a piece of the loaf, fill your cup with juice and return to your place in the circle. Wait quietly while others catch on. Then eat the bread and drink the juice.

Close with the following prayer: **God, there are so many ways you call us to act. Often we're afraid to speak up, afraid to change things that aren't right. But, like Elijah, we must stand up for your cause. Fill us with your Holy Spirit, for it's with your spiritual strength that we find the courage to bring about needed change. In Jesus' name, amen.**

Letter to the Editor

Instructions: Complete the following form and be prepared to read it to the rest of the group.

Dear Editor:
   I'm writing this letter because I'm concerned about:

Some of my concerns about this issue include:

   1.

   2.

   3.

If action isn't taken soon, I'm concerned that:

My suggestions for improving this situation would be to:

   1.

   2.

   3.

In closing, I would like to say:

                                        Sincerely,

Celebrate!

■ Theme: Celebrating God's goodness (2 Chronicles 24—33)

After Solomon's death, Israel split into two kingdoms—northern and southern. The southern kingdom, Judah, had experienced the horrible reigns of Jehoram, Ahaziah and Athaliah. It was ready for a few good years of celebration. When the boy-king Joash took over at age 7, the tide of evil changed. The priest Jehoiada influenced Joash to follow the Lord.

Joash, Amaziah, Uzziah and Jotham brought over 100 years of prosperity to Judah. After the death of Jotham, however, the power of evil returned to the royal house. Kings Ahaz, Manasseh and Amon brought corruption as they promoted the worship of foreign gods. Only King Hezekiah brought hope in the midst of these evil reigns. He put excitement back into worship for the people of Judah.

This session helps young people focus on the joy of celebration in worship and their lives.

■ Objectives

During this session participants will:
● explore 2 Chronicles 24—33;
● identify reasons to celebrate;
● create and experience a worship celebration; and
● covenant to plan a celebration for a friend or family member.

■ Preparation

Read and study 2 Chronicles 24—33 and 2 Kings 18—21.

Gather pencils, balloons (about five per person), garbage bags, Bibles, paper, hymnals and something to collect an offering in.

Cut strips of paper. Each should be small enough to roll up and fit inside a deflated balloon before blowing it up (1/2×3 inches works well).

Make one copy of the "Scripture Passage Cards" page. Cut the passages apart and tape each one to a 3×5 card. If you have more than 36 kids, duplicate some of the passages.

Make a copy of the "Action Covenant" and "Kingo Bingo" handout for each person.

Write the following order of worship (or one you design) on newsprint.
- Call to Worship (Psalm 100)
- Prayer of Thanksgiving (Psalm 46:1-3)
- Prayer of Confession (Psalm 25:8-15)
- Assurance of Pardon (Psalm 16:9-11)
- Scripture Readings (your choice)
- One-Minute Response to the Statement: "Celebration is important in my life because . . ."
- Hymn
- Offering

Prepare a cake large enough for your group. You will also need plates, forks and napkins.

The Session

■ Dig

Hand each person several strips of paper and a pencil. Say: **Today we're focusing on celebrations. On each strip of paper, write a cause to celebrate. For example, you might write the word "Spring" or "Fridays." You might also write a phrase such as "Getting an A on my test" or "My dad's new promotion." Fill out as many strips as you can.**

After kids have finished, hand out the balloons. Have kids roll up their strips of paper, place each one inside a different balloon, blow up each balloon and tie it. Collect the balloons in garbage bags and put them aside for later. Ask:
- **What was the greatest celebration you had this year?**
- **What happened this week that you could celebrate?**
- **What happens when we look for little reasons to celebrate, not just big ones?**

■ Discover

Say: **In the past, Judah had endured many bad kings. The people often had little reason to celebrate. But during the period covered in 2 Chronicles, Judah had a succession of good kings. The people celebrated their good fortune. But the greatest celebration came during King Hezekiah's reign. He called Judah back to God by re-establishing the temple worship.**

Give each person a pencil and a Bible, and distribute the "Scripture Passage Cards." Say: **Look up your scripture passages and become familiar with the king involved and what was happening. When everyone is finished, we'll play ''Kingo Bingo'' with**

these kings.

Give each person a "Kingo Bingo" handout. Say: **Each of you has researched at least one of the passages listed on this page. In the square that lists the passage you researched, write the king's name and one word to remind you of what that scripture passage was about.**

Ask the people around the room to write the name of the king they read about and a one-word reminder in the appropriate square of your "Kingo Bingo" handout. Find people with scripture passages that will complete your Bingo. When you complete six spaces in a row in any direction, yell "Kingo Bingo."

Play the game. When someone has a Bingo, check the handout against the "Kingo Bingo Leader's Sheet" to see if it's correct. After two or three people Bingo, have all kids quickly tell about their scripture passages in order.

■ Experience

Say: **Celebrating is important. Each week the celebration of worship encourages us to act as agents of God's grace in the world. Worship creates some of our most celebrated moments.**

Today we'll create our own worship celebration. We'll work in teams to design different parts of a worship experience. Complete your team's assignment, and then we'll celebrate together.

Tape the order of worship on the wall. Allow group members to choose a part of the service they'd like to work on and form teams. Give each team paper.

After 15 minutes, have all groups meet together and celebrate worship.

■ Grow

Say: **It's easy to forget how important worship is to our lives. When the kings of Judah brought the people back to God through a worship celebration, prosperity followed. If we allow worship to motivate us each week, the good news of God's presence in our lives will make our daily journeys quite different.**

Ask:

● **What's your favorite part of the worship service?**

● **What's the most difficult part of worship for you?**

● **What can you suggest to make worship more meaningful for you?**

● **What reasons for celebration do you have in your life?**

● **How does worship become your link to God?**

■ Covenant

Give each person an "Action Covenant." Have kids pair up and talk about their covenants. Have kids each talk about one way they can help their partner carry out his or her covenant. Encourage everyone to plan how and when that can happen. Have pairs each schedule a time to call or meet during the week.

■ Go

Gather everyone in a circle. Say: **On "go," I'll empty the bags of balloons. Keep them all in the air and don't break them.**

Ask volunteers to help you empty the bags. Signal the group to begin. After a few minutes, say: **Now pop the balloons and pick up the pieces of paper inside.**

After all the balloons are popped, have group members sit in a circle and take turns reading the causes for celebration written earlier. Close with a prayer of celebration for all the good things.

Serve the cake to celebrate the joy of your group working together.

Kingo Bingo Leader's Sheet

2 Chronicles 24:1-3 Joash Joash becomes king of Judah at age 7 and reigns for 40 years.	**2 Chronicles 25:25-28** Amaziah Amaziah flees to Lachish for safety, but the people from Jerusalem hunt him down and murder him.	**2 Chronicles 31:20-21** Hezekiah Hezekiah remains faithful to God and prospers.	**2 Chronicles 28:16-27** Ahaz Ahaz uses the temple treasury to buy help from the Assyrian king in a battle against the Edomites.	**2 Chronicles 29:31-36** Hezekiah The people bring their sacrifices to the temple, and everyone rejoices at what God had done for his people.	**2 Chronicles 32:20-23** Hezekiah Hezekiah and the prophet Isaiah pray for deliverance, and an angel annihilates the Assyrian army.
2 Chronicles 29:1-11 Hezekiah Hezekiah becomes king at 25 and reigns 29 years. He's a good king.	**2 Chronicles 33:1-9** Manasseh Manasseh becomes king at 12 and reigns 55 years. He rebuilds the altars to Baal and sacrifices his sons.	**2 Chronicles 24:4-14** Joash Joash taxes his people and uses the money to repair the temple.	**2 Chronicles 31:1-19** Hezekiah Idol worship centers are destroyed. Hezekiah and his people tithe to support the priesthood.	**2 Chronicles 33:18-20** Manasseh Manasseh dies.	**2 Chronicles 26:22-23** Uzziah Uzziah dies.
2 Kings 21:10-15 Manasseh Because of Manasseh's evil, the prophet predicts Jerusalem's doom.	**2 Chronicles 29:12-19** Hezekiah The Levites are consecrated and the temple is purified for worship.	**2 Chronicles 26:1-5** Uzziah Uzziah becomes king at 16 and reigns 52 years. He's loyal to God as long as Zechariah is priest.	**2 Chronicles 27:1-8** Jotham Jotham becomes king at 25 and reigns 16 years. He's a good king who builds new cities and forts.	**2 Chronicles 26:16-21** Uzziah Uzziah grows so proud that he takes over the sacred role of priest. God strikes the king with leprosy.	
2 Chronicles 32:24-26 Hezekiah When Hezekiah becomes gravely ill, he prays for a miracle. The Lord responds with a miraculous sign.	**2 Chronicles 24:17-22** Joash After Jehoiada's death, Joash begins to worship idols.	**2 Chronicles 29:20-30** Hezekiah Hezekiah and his officials make a special offering in the temple. Then they worship the Lord.	**2 Chronicles 32:27-31** Hezekiah Hezekiah grows rich and prosperous.	**2 Chronicles 28:5-15** Ahaz Because Ahaz is evil, he's defeated by the Arameans and the king of Israel. Many Judeans are killed in the battles.	**2 Chronicles 25:5-13** Amaziah Amaziah hires Israelites to help in a war against the Edomites. But God tells him to send them home.
2 Chronicles 32:16-19 Hezekiah The Assyrian king continues to insult God and Hezekiah by writing frightening letters to the people.	**2 Chronicles 33:21-25** Amon Amon becomes king at 22 and reigns two years. He refuses to obey God and is killed by his officials.	**2 Chronicles 33:14-17** Manasseh Manasseh removes all the altars he built and tells the people to serve the Lord and worship in the temple again.	**2 Chronicles 24:23-27** Joash A small Aramean army conquers the Judean army and wounds Joash. Later Joash is murdered.	**2 Chronicles 25:1-4** Amaziah Amaziah becomes king at 25 and reigns 29 years. He's faithful to God for most of his reign.	**2 Chronicles 33:10-13** Manasseh Manasseh refuses to listen to God. But after he's captured by the Assyrians, he cries out to God for deliverance.
2 Chronicles 25:14-24 Amaziah Amaziah brings idols back to Judah as spoils of victory and begins to worship them, angering the Lord.	**2 Chronicles 32:1-15** Hezekiah The Assyrian army invades Judah and tells the people to turn away from the Lord to save themselves.	**2 Chronicles 32:32-33** Hezekiah Hezekiah dies.	**2 Chronicles 26:6-15** Uzziah Uzziah defeats the Philistines, strengthens the defense of Jerusalem and organizes a well-trained army.	**2 Chronicles 30:13-27** Hezekiah Many people celebrate the Passover. The festival continues for seven days.	**2 Chronicles 30:1-12** Hezekiah Hezekiah invites Judah and Israel to celebrate Passover in the temple. Many Israelites scorn the invitation.
					2 Chronicles 28:1-4 Ahaz Ahaz becomes king at 20 and reigns 16 years. He's an evil king who sacrifices his sons to idols.

Kingo Bingo

2 Chronicles 24:1-3	2 Chronicles 25:25-28	2 Chronicles 31:20-21	2 Chronicles 28:16-27	2 Chronicles 29:31-36	2 Chronicles 32:20-23
2 Chronicles 29:1-11	2 Chronicles 33:1-9	2 Chronicles 24:4-14	2 Chronicles 31:1-19	2 Chronicles 33:18-20	2 Chronicles 26:22-23
2 Kings 21:10-15	2 Chronicles 29:12-19	2 Chronicles 26:1-5	2 Chronicles 27:1-8	2 Chronicles 28:5-15	2 Chronicles 25:5-13
2 Chronicles 32:24-26	2 Chronicles 24:17-22	2 Chronicles 29:20-30	2 Chronicles 32:27-31	2 Chronicles 26:16-21	2 Chronicles 33:10-13
2 Chronicles 32:16-19	2 Chronicles 33:21-25	2 Chronicles 33:14-17	2 Chronicles 24:23-27	2 Chronicles 25:1-4	2 Chronicles 30:1-12
2 Chronicles 25:14-24	2 Chronicles 32:1-15	2 Chronicles 32:32-33	2 Chronicles 26:6-15	2 Chronicles 30:13-27	2 Chronicles 28:1-4

Scripture Passage Cards

Instructions: Cut apart these scripture references and tape each onto a different 3×5 card.

2 Chronicles 24:1-3	2 Chronicles 24:4-14	2 Chronicles 24:17-22
2 Chronicles 24:23-27	2 Chronicles 25:1-4	2 Chronicles 25:5-13
2 Chronicles 25:14-24	2 Chronicles 25:25-28	2 Chronicles 26:1-5
2 Chronicles 26:6-15	2 Chronicles 26:16-21	2 Chronicles 26:22-23
2 Chronicles 27:1-8	2 Chronicles 28:1-4	2 Chronicles 28:5-15
2 Chronicles 28:16-27	2 Chronicles 29:1-11	2 Chronicles 29:12-19
2 Chronicles 29:20-30	2 Chronicles 29:31-36	2 Chronicles 30:1-12
2 Chronicles 30:13-27	2 Chronicles 31:1-19	2 Chronicles 31:20-21
2 Chronicles 32:1-15	2 Chronicles 32:16-19	2 Chronicles 32:20-23
2 Chronicles 32:24-26	2 Chronicles 32:27-31	2 Chronicles 32:32-33
2 Chronicles 33:1-9	2 Chronicles 33:10-13	2 Chronicles 33:14-17
2 Chronicles 33:18-20	2 Kings 21:10-15	2 Chronicles 33:21-25

Action Covenant

A friend or family member who needs to experience a celebration is . . .

One celebration I could secretly plan for this person would be . . .

The people I'd need to help me plan are . . .

I'll begin to make plans for this surprise celebration this week. The first step I'll take is . . .

Signed . . . .
Witness . . . .
Date . . . .

Starting From Scratch

■ Theme: Starting over (Ezra, Nehemiah, Haggai, Zechariah)

The time of the good kings was past. The temple and the walls of Jerusalem had lain in ruins for 70 years and the Jews had lived in captivity in Babylon since 587 B.C. Then the powerful Persian army conquered Babylon. Mercifully, King Cyrus of Persia let the Jews go home to Jerusalem.

Ezra and Nehemiah detail the Israelites' return to Jerusalem following the captivity. The books of Haggai and Zechariah contain prophetic encouragement to Israel during Jerusalem's reconstruction.

Rebuilding is a part of life. But as teenagers work to rebuild their lives after a tragedy or major disappointment, frustration and impatience take their toll. This session offers hope for kids who feel their lives have reached a dead end.

■ Objectives

During this session participants will:
- explore the themes of Ezra, Nehemiah, Haggai and Zechariah;
- rate the distress caused by various starting-over situations;
- discuss the rebuilding of Jerusalem and the temple;
- discuss people's needs during rebuilding times; and
- covenant to support someone who's starting over.

■ Preparation

Scan Ezra, Nehemiah, Haggai and Zechariah.

Gather Bibles, pencils and a package of flower seeds.

Write each of the following headings on a separate sheet of newsprint: "Great Difficulty" and "Little Difficulty." Hang the sheets at opposite ends of the meeting area.

Make a copy of the "Scripture Dig" handout and the "Action Covenant" for each person.

Gather seven wooden building-blocks from your church nursery for each person, or cut 2×4 boards into 6-inch lengths.

Buy or borrow a recording of Billy Crockett's song "Time to Begin Again" from his *Carrier* album (Word). You'll also need a stereo. If you're unable to find this song use another "fresh start" song.

The Session

■ Dig

Say: **Today we're going to talk about starting over. Assume our room is a long line. On one end you see the words "Great Difficulty," and on the other end you read "Little Difficulty." These are the two extremes. I'm going to read several situations. Stand somewhere between these two points in relation to how tough it would be to start over in each situation.**

Read the following statements and let the kids respond to each one by choosing a spot between the signs. After each response, ask kids why they stood where they did.

Situations:

- **You and your boyfriend/girlfriend break up after dating for a year**
- **Your parents divorce**
- **You move to a new city**
- **Your best friend moves away**
- **You move and have to change schools**
- **You graduate from high school and face college**
- **You're permanently blinded in a car accident**
- **You fail a required course and must take it over**
- **Your family dies in a car accident and you're left alone**
- **Your house burns down, and you lose everything you own**

After discussing the situations, ask:

- **Why is it so hard to face starting-over times?**
- **Of all the things you just responded to, which two would be the hardest? Why?**

■ Discover

Say: **The Jews faced a difficult rebuilding time. When Persia conquered Babylon, King Cyrus let the Jews return to Jerusalem. They'd been living in captivity for 70 years. Four books of the Old Testament contain the story of their return: Ezra, Nehemiah, Haggai and Zechariah.**

Form three groups. Give a "Scripture Dig" handout, Bible and pencil to each person. Assign a section of the handout to each group. Have kids each discuss their answers in their group. While groups are working, lay out the wooden blocks.

■ Experience

When groups finish, give each person seven blocks. Say: **We're** going to work together to build the wall of Jerusalem and the temple. Each block represents a different event you read about. For each block, decide how you'd complete the statement "This block represents the time when . . ." For example, someone from group #1 might say: "This block represents the edict from Cyrus that let the Hebrews return home. This second block represents the gold and silver they were given when they left for home." Group #1 will build the temple, groups #2 and #3 will build the wall around it.

Bring the groups together and have them build together. Then ask:
- How did you feel as the temple walls took shape?
- What do you think it meant to the Jews to go home?
- Why did the Jews refuse the Samaritans' help?
- If you'd been a Hebrew with a foreign wife would you have been willing to give her up? Why or why not?
- Why was it so critical to return to the law given at Mount Sinai?

∎ Grow

Say: **No one enjoys starting over. But those times happen. No one is immune. Billy Crockett has a great song about starting over. It's called "Time to Begin Again."**

Play the song, and discuss it. Then ask:
- What does Christ call us to do for others who are starting over?
- What keeps you from letting others help you when you face dead-end times?
- How has God helped you during those times?
- What's the most difficult starting-over experience you've had? How did you deal with it? Who helped?
- Who do you know who's facing a rebuilding time? What could you do to help?

∎ Covenant

Hand out and have kids complete the "Action Covenant."

∎ Go

Gather everyone in a circle. Share a personal story reflecting a starting-over time. Ask others to share their starting-over stories. Pass around a handful of flower seeds. Ask how they represent hope for starting over.

Pray: **God, it's really hard to start over. Sometimes we don't know who to turn to or how to cope. Help us during those times. Give us peace. Help us encourage others facing tough times. In Jesus' name, amen.**

Scripture Dig

Group #1: Rebuilding the Temple

1. What was Cyrus' edict (Ezra 1:1-4)?

2. What did Cyrus give the Jews to take with them (Ezra 1:7-10)?

3. How many people returned (Ezra 2:64-67)?

4. What was the first thing the people did when they returned (Ezra 3:1-3)?

5. When did work on the temple begin (Ezra 3:8-9)?

6. When was the temple finished (Ezra 6:15)?

7. What difficult reform did Ezra carry out (Ezra 10:10-17)?

Group #2: Rebuilding the Wall

1. What news was brought to Nehemiah (Nehemiah 1:1-3)?

2. What does Nehemiah request (Nehemiah 2:1-8)?

3. What does Nehemiah want to do for Jerusalem (Nehemiah 2:17)?

4. What success does Nehemiah have (Nehemiah 4:6)?

5. How does Nehemiah face the opposition (Nehemiah 4:7-23)?

6. What does Nehemiah do about wealth and poverty (Nehemiah 5:1-13)?

7. How does Nehemiah serve as an example to the people (Nehemiah 5:14-18)?

Group #3: Encouraging the People

1. How did the people respond to Haggai's encouragement (Haggai 1:13-15)?

2. What is Zechariah's promise for Jerusalem (Zechariah 1:14, 16-17)?

3. What does Zechariah say is the reason God didn't deliver his people from captivity earlier (Zechariah 7:8-13)?

4. What does Zechariah say is God's plan for Jerusalem (Zechariah 8:3-5, 12)?

5. What does Zechariah say will be the ultimate status of Jerusalem in the world (Zechariah 8:20-23)?

Action Covenant

Someone I know who's going through a rebuilding time is . . .

He or she is facing the hard task of . . .

The ways I could support this person are . . .

I covenant to support this person in the coming week by . . .

Signed . . . .
Witness . . . .
Date . . . .

The Queen and I

■ Theme: Facing peer pressure (Esther)

The Jews had rebuilt the temple and Jerusalem. Many, however, had settled in Persia and didn't return to their homeland. A Jewish girl became queen of Persia and averted a plot to destroy her people.

The book of Esther tells how Queen Esther discovered a plot by Haman, the king's right-hand man, to kill all the Jews in Persia. With the help of Mordecai, her cousin, Esther risked the king's disapproval to ask him to stop the plot and save her people. In the end the Jews had a two-day celebration called the Feast of Purim.

Peer pressure strongly affects teenagers today. This session helps teenagers make decisions based on their beliefs rather than give in to peer pressure.

■ Objectives

During this session participants will:
- study the book of Esther;
- discuss how peer pressure affects them;
- perform a reader's theater of the story of Esther; and
- discuss effective/ineffective ways of dealing with peer pressure.

■ Preparation

Read and study the book of Esther.

Gather pencils and a small package of sugar and a small package of pepper for each person. Make a copy of "The Queen and I" and "Pressure Poll" handouts for each person.

Write the following phrases on pieces of paper and tape them randomly on walls around the meeting area:
- TV ads
- loud-speaking people
- fast pace
- hard teachers
- parents
- logic
- fear of punishment
- magazine ads
- soft-speaking people
- slow pace
- easy teachers
- peer group
- feelings
- promised reward

The Session

■ Dig

Say: **Every day we make choices. Someone's trying to persuade us one way or the other. For each pair of choices I give you, choose the one that would probably pressure you the most, and go stand by your choice wherever it is in the room.**

Read these choices one at a time. Discuss kids' choices as you go.

I am more pressured by . . .

- **TV ads or magazine ads**
- **Loud-speaking or soft-speaking people**
- **Fast pace or slow pace**
- **Hard or easy teachers**
- **Parents or peer group**
- **Logic or feelings**
- **Fear of punishment or promised reward**

Ask:

- **Are you easily pressured? Why or why not?**
- **How effective are you at persuading others? Explain.**

■ Discover

Say: **We're going to study the book of Esther today. Esther was a Jewish girl who didn't return to Jerusalem with the other Jews after their captivity. She became queen in Persia around 486 B.C. While queen, she discovered a horrible plot to exterminate all the Jews in Persia.**

Give everyone a copy of the handout "The Queen and I." Assign parts for Esther, Mordecai, Haman and King Xerxes. Assign the rest of the group to act as the narrator, reading in unison.

Have kids stand in a circle, facing each other. Tell kids this is a reader's theater. They are to remain still, using only their voices and facial expressions to convey the character. Begin the reading.

After the reader's theater, ask:

- **Was Mordecai right in refusing to bow down? Why or why not?**
- **What would you have done in Mordecai's place?**
- **What kind of pressure did Esther use on the king?** (Read Esther 5:1-8; 7:1-10)
- **Why was Esther willing to risk her life?**
- **What other methods might Esther have used to stop Haman's plot? What might've happened?**
- **Why was the king so receptive to Esther?**

■ Experience

Say: **I'm going to give you a "Pressure Poll." It contains several statements that describe different forms of peer pressure. Complete the form on your own.**

Distribute the "Pressure Poll" handouts and pencils, and let kids mark their responses. After kids have completed the handouts, have them pair up. Assign each pair one statement from the "Pressure Poll." Tell pairs each to design a one-minute skit to persuade other group members in the style of their statement. For example, the pair with the statement "Bribery is useful" could try to bribe the rest of the group to see their point of view. They might do that by offering money, friendship or the like.

After five minutes of preparation, bring the pairs together and have them share the one-minute presentations. Ask:

● **How does peer pressure affect your life?**

● **What kind of peer pressure do you give in to most often? least often?**

■ Grow

Say: **As Christians we're called to invite others to follow Christ. That means we must have Christlike motives as we deal with others.**

Ask:

● **Can Christians use pressure to Christ's advantage? If so, is it right?**

● **Why is it sometimes difficult to make wise decisions when with non-Christian friends?**

● **Does peer pressure sometimes help us do the right things? Explain.**

● **What can we do to prepare for times when friends pressure us to do wrong?**

● **How can we invite others to Christ without pressuring them?**

■ Go

Gather everyone in a circle. Pass around the packages of sugar and pepper. Say: **Peer pressure usually comes in packages just like these—one sugar, one pepper. Both change the flavor but how they do it is vastly different. What's the difference?**

(For example, one person might say sugar is like the peer pressure that makes you feel good after you make a change for the better. Pepper on the other hand, might leave you in a hot spot after using it.)

Pray that Christ will dwell richly in each person and will give kids courage and wisdom like Esther and Mordecai.

The Queen and I

Characters: Esther (pronounced Es-ter), Mordecai (pronounced Mor-dek-eye), Haman (pronounced Hey-mun), King Xerxes (pronounced Zerk-zees), Narrator

Narrator: King Xerxes honored Haman by giving him authority over all the other nobles. All the nobles knelt down to Haman when they saw him, because the king told them to. But Mordecai wouldn't kneel down or honor Haman in any way. When Haman saw that Mordecai wouldn't kneel down before him, he was enraged. Haman not only wanted Mordecai killed, but he also wanted to slaughter every Jew in Persia. So Haman went to the king and said,

Haman: King Xerxes, the Jews don't obey your laws. Why don't you decree that all the Jews be killed so we can make an example of them?

King Xerxes: Okay.

Narrator: And so Haman set out to destroy the Jews. Soon, Mordecai heard of Haman's plot, and he was really upset. He put on sackcloth and poured ashes on his head. Queen Esther, a cousin of Mordecai and also a Jew, asked why he was so upset. When Esther found out, she too was distressed. Mordecai told her,

Mordecai: Do not think that because you are the Queen you will escape. For if you remain silent, deliverance for the Jews will arise from another place, but you and your father's family will perish. And who knows? Maybe you have come to a royal position just for such a time as this.

Narrator: So Esther said to Mordecai,

Esther: Gather together all the Jews and fast for three days. Then I will go to the king, even though it's against the law. And if I perish, I perish.

Narrator: So Mordecai gathered all the Jews and they fasted. On the third day, Esther went into the king's royal chamber. If—when the king saw Esther—he didn't hold out his golden scepter, then Esther would be killed. Fortunately, the king liked Esther and held out his scepter. The king said,

King Xerxes: What's up?

Esther: I want you and Haman to come to a banquet I've prepared.

King Xerxes: Okay. Sounds good to me!

Narrator: So the king and Haman came and ate at Esther's banquet. And the king asked Esther a second time,

King Xerxes: What's up?

Esther: I'll tell you if you come to a banquet I'll prepare for you tomorrow.

continued

King: Okay.

Narrator: That night the king couldn't sleep, so he had a servant read to him the records of his reign. King Xerxes discovered that Mordecai had once saved his life, but had never been honored for it. Just about that time, Haman came in. King Xerxes asked him,

King Xerxes: What should I do for someone I really want to honor?

Narrator: Now Haman thought the king was talking about him.

Haman: Well, you should put him in the king's best clothes and parade him around town on a great horse. And you should have someone yell, "This is how the king honors a man he really likes."

King Xerxes: Good idea! Tomorrow, I want you to do that for Mordecai.

Narrator: Boy, was Haman mad! But he did as the king ordered. After Mordecai paraded through the streets, Haman rushed off to Esther's second banquet. While Haman and the king were eating, the king asked Esther a third time,

King Xerxes: Now really. What's up?

Esther: Okay, I'll tell you. There's a man in your government who has sentenced me and all my people to death. And I'm not too happy about it.

King Xerxes: Who?

Esther: The evil Haman.

Narrator: When the king heard this, he was furious. He left the banquet hall in a rage. Haman was terrified. So he begged Esther for his life.

Haman: Pleeeze! O, come on, pleeeeze!

Narrator: After the king had taken a brisk walk, he returned to the banquet hall, only to find Haman falling onto the couch where Esther was reclining. The king yelled,

King Xerxes: How dare you!

Haman: Oops!

Narrator: The king had Haman hung the next morning. Then the king revoked the law that called for all the Jews to be killed. He gave Mordecai Haman's old job, and the Jews had a great feast that they still celebrate to this day. The end.

Pressure Poll

Instructions: Read each statement and check whether it is true or false for you.

	True	False
1. When someone threatens me I don't let it change my behavior.	_____	_____
2. If you're right, it's okay to use a little deceit to persuade people to your side.	_____	_____
3. I tend to give in to people who continually pester me to do something I don't want to do.	_____	_____
4. I think people should always be blunt and straight about their feelings. No matter what.	_____	_____
5. The use of gentleness and kindness doesn't get you very far.	_____	_____
6. "Sweet talk" always helps loosen up people when you want them to do something.	_____	_____
7. Sometimes harmless manipulation is necessary to produce positive peer-pressure.	_____	_____
8. To get ahead in life you have to fit in with the crowd.	_____	_____
9. Bribery is useful in pressuring people.	_____	_____
10. I like to send people on a guilt trip when they don't do what I want.	_____	_____

Hanging Tough

■ Theme: Dealing with suffering (Job)

The book of Job has received frequent attention from Old Testament readers. We find a man of wealth who suddenly encountered suffering. His possessions were wiped out, his family killed and his body ravaged by disease.

The book focuses on conversations between Job and his friends, who gave Job answers to his questions—answers that never seemed adequate. In the end Job's conversation with God finally brought the truth.

Teenagers experience and struggle to be patient in suffering. This session helps kids explore the theme of suffering and discuss the tough questions they have on this perplexing issue.

■ Objectives

During this session participants will:
● reflect on the message of the book of Job;
● discuss ways people suffer;
● explore reasons for suffering and ways Christians can help alleviate it; and
● write cards of hope to people who are suffering.

■ Preparation

Scan the book of Job.

Gather construction paper, markers, masking tape, five sheets of posterboard and Bibles. Make a copy of the "Scripture Dig" and "Real People" handouts for each person.

If possible, get a copy of Ann Weems' book *Reaching for Rainbows* (Westminster Press).

The Session

■ Dig

Say: **Today we're going to talk about suffering. Everyone suffers in one way or another at some time. Suffering comes in many forms. Let's identify some.**

Place the construction paper, markers and masking tape in the center of the room. Ask participants each to take a sheet of construction paper and write an example of a form of suffering they've seen. For example, they may write poverty, racial prejudice or cancer. Have them tape their sheets on the wall.

Discuss the kinds of suffering they listed. Ask:

- **When was a time you suffered?**
- **Why is there so much suffering in life?**

■ Discover

Say: **The book of Job deals with suffering. Here we find a good man who encountered one disaster after another. He lost his possessions, his family and his health. His friends tried to convince him he must have done something wrong, or the tragedy wouldn't have happened. Finally, Job encountered God, who helped him find answers.**

Give each person a "Scripture Dig" handout, and assign eight readers for the parts. If you have fewer than eight people, assign some kids more than one part each. Go through the reading. When the reading is over, ask:

- **Why did Job's friends fail to help him?**
- **How would you have reacted if they had been your friends?**
- **Why did Job decide he wanted to die?**
- **How do you feel about his decision?**
- **What or who do you think causes suffering in the world? Why?**

■ Experience

Form five groups. Hand each group a sheet of posterboard and markers. Instruct each group to fold its posterboard in half to shape it into a card.

Give a copy of the "Real People" handout to each group. Have each group choose a different situation and create a card of hope to the person in that situation.

Bring the groups together and have them share their cards. Ask:

- **What was difficult about creating your card?**

● **How do you feel about the person you made the card for?**

● **Who is suffering most in our world? Why?**

● **How can Christians bring hope to those who suffer?**

■ Grow

Say: **It's difficult getting through times of suffering. In the Bible we discover that hope in the midst of suffering comes only through God.**

Create a continuum across the room by assigning one end of the meeting area to represent "10" and the opposite end to represent "1." Explain that you're going to ask kids to answer the next question by moving to the spot they choose on the continuum. Then ask:

● **On a scale of 1 to 10, with 10 being maximum suffering, where would you rate the level of suffering you've experienced so far in your life?**

Once the kids have positioned themselves along the continuum, ask:

● **Was it difficult to choose a spot on the continuum? Why or why not?**

● **How much did other people influence your choice? Explain.**

● **Does suffering stem more from poor circumstances or a poor attitude? Explain.**

Form groups of four. Read each question aloud, and have kids each respond in their groups:

● **What's one time you experienced suffering?**

● **How have you learned to survive rough times?**

● **Do you think God is punishing you with suffering?**

● **How do you think Jesus provides for you in times of suffering?**

● **How do you think following Christ can cause us to suffer?** (Read Luke 9:23-24)

■ Go

Gather everyone in a circle. Share a time when you faced suffering. Ask others to share their stories about suffering. Read the poem "I'd Write for You a Rainbow" from the book *Reaching for Rainbows*. Ask kids what the poem means to them.

If you don't have the book, ask the group to choose someone in your church who has recently endured suffering. Decide as a group how you could give a "rainbow of love" to that person. For example, the group might take a fresh bouquet of flowers to a church member who has just had surgery.

Close the session with the following prayer: **God, we can't avoid all suffering in our lives. Help us face suffering with courage** and faith, and look to you to get us through. Help us reach out this week to someone who's suffering and bring your love to that person. In Jesus' name, amen.

Scripture Dig

Instructions: Assign these characters—Narrator, Lord, Satan, Job, Eliphaz, Bildad, Zophar and Elihu. Then have characters read in order the passages listed below.

1. Narrator—Job 1:1-4, 6

2. Lord—Job 1:7a

3. Satan—Job 1:7b

4. Lord—Job 1:8

5. Satan—Job 1:9-11

6. Lord—Job 1:12

7. Narrator—Job 1:13-20

8. Job—Job 1:21

9. Narrator—Job 1:22; 2:1

10. Lord—Job 2:2a

11. Satan—Job 2:2b

12. Lord—Job 2:3

13. Satan—Job 2:4-5

14. Lord—Job 2:6

15. Narrator—Job 2:7, 11-13

16. Job—Job 12:4

17. Eliphaz—Job 15:12-16

18. Job—Job 16:1-3

19. Bildad—Job 18:2-4

20. Job—Job 19:1-7, 21-22

21. Zophar—Job 20:4-9

22. Job—Job 27:5-6

23. Narrator—Job 32:1-6

24. Elihu—Job 33:8-28

25. Narrator—Job 38:1

26. Lord—Job 38:2-12; 40:1-2

27. Job—Job 40:3-5

28. Lord—Job 40:7-14

29. Job—Job 42:1-6

30. Narrator—Job 42:10-12

Real People

1. An AIDS patient

2. A homeless person

3. A severely handicapped person

4. A rape victim

5. A friend with an alcoholic parent

6. A terminal cancer patient

7. A political prisoner

8. A person in a country ruled by a cruel and powerful dictator

9. A poor person living in low-income housing

10. Your parent who has just been phased out of his or her job

Heart Songs

■ Theme: Giving thanks and praise (Psalms)

Several themes fill the Psalms: praise, thanksgiving, wisdom, personal and national sorrow, deliverance. All facets of life are displayed in the Psalms.

The Psalms help us understand life and our relationship with God. They bring us comfort, hope and promise. They lift us up in the midst of our despair and bring words of praise to our lips. They become a bridge to God.

This session examines the themes of thanksgiving and praise. It helps kids focus on God's beauty and majesty.

■ Objectives

During this session participants will:
● explore the major themes of the Psalms;
● write psalms related to specific themes;
● discuss opinions on prayer as they relate to the Psalms; and
● covenant to include praise in their lives.

■ Preparation

Read and study the following Psalms: 8, 19, 23, 40, 73, 96, 100, 121, 146. Make notes on any insights.

Gather Bibles, papers, markers, newsprint and a cassette player or record player.

On a sheet of newsprint write the following questions and tape the sheet on the wall:

1. What is the Psalm's theme?
2. What is the psalmist trying to say?
3. How does the Psalm relate to your life?

Make a copy of the "Action Covenant" for each person.

Buy or borrow a recording of "The Lord Is My Shepherd (23rd Psalm)" from Keith Green's *The Ministry Years 1980-1982, Volume 2* (Sparrow). If you can't obtain this record, find another version of Psalm 23.

The Session

■ Dig

Say: **I want your opinions about praise and thanksgiving. When I read a statement, express your feeling this way: strongly agree, both thumbs up; agree, one thumb up; not sure, level hand; disagree, one thumb down; strongly disagree, both thumbs down.**

Read each statement. Let each person vote, then discuss the statement.

1. You should express praise to God every day.

2. God wants us to be thankful for everything that happens to us.

3. We should spend more time praising God than asking God to meet our needs.

4. God enjoys our praise.

5. We can praise God in many ways.

6. Giving thanks is often difficult.

7. We must include praise and thanksgiving every time we pray.

8. Praise increases our understanding of God.

9. We feel closer to God when we spend time thanking him for all he has done.

10. We should spend time praising and thanking God before we pray about anything else.

■ Discover

Say: **Psalms is a big book. Today we'll look at several Psalms that cover major themes.**

Give each person a piece of paper and a marker. Assign at least one of the following Psalms to each person: 8, 19, 23, 40, 73, 96, 100, 121, 146. Ask kids each to read their Psalm and answer on their paper the questions on the newsprint. Bring the kids together and have them share their discoveries. Ask:

● **How did you relate to the Psalm you read?**

● **Why do you think the Psalms are so personal?**

● **What do you appreciate most about the Psalms?**

● **What is your favorite Psalm? Why?**

■ Experience

Say: **The Psalms are personal expressions of individuals' faith. Today we're going to experience that same kind of personal expression by writing our own psalms.**

Break into groups of four to six (a group can be one person). Hand each group newsprint and a marker. Assign one of the following themes to each group:

- A psalm of praise (example: Psalm 8)
- A psalm of thanks (example: Psalm 9:1-6)
- A psalm of deliverance (example: Psalm 25:16-22)
- A psalm of personal reflection (example: Psalm 23)
- A psalm of hope (example: Psalm 46)

Have groups each write a five- to 10-verse psalm built around their theme. Challenge each group to present its psalm dramatically. Tell the groups that they can use lighting, props and any style of presentation they want, but they must stay in the room.

Bring the groups together and have them share their psalms. Ask:

- **How do psalms help us express our feelings?**
- **What were you trying to express to God?**
- **How are psalms like prayers? like songs?**

Say: **Here's Psalm 23 put to music.**

Play "The Lord Is My Shepherd (23rd Psalm)" from the Keith Green album.

Ask:

When you hear this Psalm put to music, how does that change how you feel about it?

Have everyone read the Psalm aloud as a group.

■ Grow

Say: **The Psalms help us understand our feelings and express ourselves to God.**

Ask:

- **What part of your life experience was reflected in the Psalm you studied earlier?**
- **How can the Psalms help your prayer life?**
- **What would it mean to say Psalm 23 as a prayer?**
- **How can you grow closer to God by using the Psalms?**

■ Covenant

Say: **Praise and thanksgiving are important for Christians. Without them we lose sight of God's greatness and forget what he has done for us.**

Hand out and have kids complete the "Action Covenant."

■ Go

Get a Bible and take the group outside (if weather permits). Sit in a circle together in a comfortable place. Turn to Psalm 8. Read one line at a time, and ask the group to repeat it back to you. Ask kids to look around at God's creation. Ask:

What does it mean to hear the words: "You made him a little lower than the heavenly beings"?

Send the group out to collect some object of nature from the surrounding area. Caution kids not to damage anything. When everyone returns, ask:

How does your object relate to the statement in Psalm 8 that we were made rulers over all things?

Go around the circle and have each person respond.

Share this prayer: **Dear God, your creation's beauty surrounds us. You have given it to us to enjoy. Thank you. Help us to love each other as you have loved us. Help us to sing psalms of praise to you. Help us never forget that you have given us Jesus Christ so we can live abundant lives. In his name, amen.**

Action Covenant

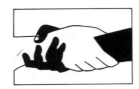

One thing God has done in my life that I could praise him for is . . .

One thing I am thankful for that I have not shared with God recently is . . .

I covenant this week to begin praising God more often by . . .

Signed . . . .
Witness . . . .
Date . . . .

What Builds Character?

■ Theme: Building character (Proverbs)

Solomon asked God for the gift of wisdom. The book of Proverbs contains much of that wisdom. The book became an instruction manual on character.

Proverbs contains straightforward advice about sin and dishonesty, and a call to follow life's virtues. The first chapter contains the book's theme: "The fear of the Lord is the beginning of knowledge."

This session helps kids understand what it takes to build good character and helps them develop a desire for wise living.

■ Objectives

During this session participants will:
- discuss the major themes of Proverbs;
- take a "Character Profile" rating based on Proverbs;
- discuss important traits of good character; and
- affirm positive character traits in each other.

■ Preparation

Read the following Proverbs. Write what each means to you.
- Proverbs 1:7
- Proverbs 2:1-8, 16-19
- Proverbs 3:5-6, 33-34
- Proverbs 6:6-19
- Proverbs 10:18-21
- Proverbs 11:22, 28
- Proverbs 13:11, 20
- Proverbs 14:15
- Proverbs 15:28
- Proverbs 16:18-19
- Proverbs 17:10, 17, 20
- Proverbs 19:17, 19
- Proverbs 22:1
- Proverbs 30:18-19, 21-23

Gather chalkboard, chalk, masking tape, markers, Bibles and construction paper.

Make a copy of the "Scripture Dig" and "Character Profile" handouts for each person.

The Session

■ Dig

Draw a line down the middle of a chalkboard. On one side put the heading "A person reveals weak character when . . ." On the other put "A person reveals strong character when . . ." Have kids each respond to the statements, and have a volunteer write the responses on the chalkboard. Then ask:

● **How would you define character?**

● **How does a person develop character?**

● **What things lead to good character development? bad character development?**

■ Discover

Say: **We're going to study several Proverbs and see what they say about building strong character.**

Give each person a Bible, "Scripture Dig" handout, construction paper and marker. Assign one or more Proverbs from the handout to each person. Say: **Look up your Proverb. Think about what it means to you, paraphrase it on a sheet of construction paper and tape the sheet on the wall.**

Ask kids each to read their Proverb from the Bible and then share their paraphrase. Ask:

● **What did the authors of Proverbs want us to learn?**

● **Why are the Proverbs still important to us?**

● **What do you like most/least about Proverbs?**

● **How can Proverbs help you understand what builds character in a person?**

● **Which Proverbs are your favorite? Why?**

■ Experience

Give each person a "Character Profile" handout. Say: **This sheet lists statements about character. Rate your own character. Be honest. We'll discuss your profiles when you're done.**

When kids are ready, have each pick their strongest character trait. Have them share their choices with the group. Ask:

● **What did you discover about the strengths of your character? about the weaknesses?**

● **How hard was it to be honest? Why?**

● **When you heard we were going to discuss your profiles, were you tempted to overstate your positive traits or understate your negative ones to make you look better? Why or why not?**

● **How does that temptation relate to strong character as seen in Proverbs?**

● **What does this exercise tell you about yourself?**

■ Grow

Say: **Character development happens every day of our lives. As a teenager, you're constantly deciding what character traits will be important for you. That's why Proverbs was written—to help people know how to do the right thing.**

Ask:

● **Who is the best model you have for developing good character? Why?**

● **Which character trait do you admire most in your mom? your dad? your favorite teacher? your best friend? yourself?**

● **What character traits do you think the disciples admired most in Jesus? In what ways did they try to become like him?**

● **What character traits do you admire most in Jesus? Which ones are important to have in your own life?**

■ Go

Gather everyone in a circle. Ask kids to write the character trait they most admire in each person on the back of that individual's profile. For example, they might list honesty, sincerity or faithfulness on the back of a person's profile. Have kids share some of the traits they listed for others.

Affirm the good character traits seen in each group member. Challenge kids to look for those same traits in their parents and friends. Challenge kids to look to Jesus as the model for character development and to continue to read and reflect on Proverbs as a source of wisdom.

Close with prayer.

Scripture Dig

Instructions: Look up your assigned Proverb, paraphrase it on a sheet of construction paper and tape the sheet on the wall.

- Proverbs 1:7
- Proverbs 2:1-8
- Proverbs 2:16-19
- Proverbs 3:5-6
- Proverbs 3:33-34
- Proverbs 6:6-15
- Proverbs 6:16-19
- Proverbs 10:18-21
- Proverbs 11:22
- Proverbs 11:28

- Proverbs 13:11
- Proverbs 13:20
- Proverbs 14:15
- Proverbs 15:28
- Proverbs 16:18-19
- Proverbs 17:10, 17, 20
- Proverbs 19:17, 19
- Proverbs 22:1
- Proverbs 30:18-19
- Proverbs 30:21-23

Character Profile

Instructions: Each character statement below is based on a theme in Proverbs. Rank each character statement as you feel it appears in your life.

Character Statement	never	always
1. I'm slow to get angry.	1 2 3 4 5 6 7 8 9 10	
2. I choose my friends wisely.	1 2 3 4 5 6 7 8 9 10	
3. I accept helpful criticism without getting huffy.	1 2 3 4 5 6 7 8 9 10	
4. I don't stir up trouble between people.	1 2 3 4 5 6 7 8 9 10	
5. I'm a generous person.	1 2 3 4 5 6 7 8 9 10	
6. I have high respect for my parents.	1 2 3 4 5 6 7 8 9 10	
7. I value a good reputation.	1 2 3 4 5 6 7 8 9 10	
8. Friendship is important to me.	1 2 3 4 5 6 7 8 9 10	
9. I always tell the truth.	1 2 3 4 5 6 7 8 9 10	
10. I place high value on my integrity.	1 2 3 4 5 6 7 8 9 10	
11. I love my neighbors.	1 2 3 4 5 6 7 8 9 10	
12. I control the words I say.	1 2 3 4 5 6 7 8 9 10	
13. I value my parent's advice.	1 2 3 4 5 6 7 8 9 10	
14. God is very important to me.	1 2 3 4 5 6 7 8 9 10	
15. I'm concerned about the poor.	1 2 3 4 5 6 7 8 9 10	
16. I don't seek revenge when wronged.	1 2 3 4 5 6 7 8 9 10	
17. I'm kind to animals.	1 2 3 4 5 6 7 8 9 10	
18. I appreciate the gifts of nature.	1 2 3 4 5 6 7 8 9 10	
19. I want to be a righteous person.	1 2 3 4 5 6 7 8 9 10	
20. I value money and use it wisely.	1 2 3 4 5 6 7 8 9 10	
21. I know humility is important.	1 2 3 4 5 6 7 8 9 10	
22. I try to speak kind words.	1 2 3 4 5 6 7 8 9 10	
23. I work hard.	1 2 3 4 5 6 7 8 9 10	

What's the Meaning of Life?

■ Theme: Enjoying life (Ecclesiastes)

"Ecclesiastes" means "The Preacher." This book focuses on tough questions that plague us. The author tells us life must be accepted as it comes—whether good or bad. Yet, he expresses hope for those who honor God with their lives. They alone have a chance for true happiness.

Teenagers often ask the question: "What's life all about?"

Discovering who we are meant to be as God's creation empowers us to live full lives. This session helps kids explore the meaning of life. It helps kids address feelings of despair and discover God's purpose for their lives.

■ Objectives

During this session participants will:
- discuss the themes of Ecclesiastes;
- list God's gifts that make life enjoyable; and
- share good and bad experiences from their lives.

■ Preparation

Scan the book of Ecclesiastes.

Gather paper, markers, Bibles and masking tape.

Make a copy of the "Scripture Dig" handout for each person.

On newsprint, draw a large tree with four large limbs but no leaves. Tape it on the wall. Label the four limbs: Material, Physical, Emotional, Spiritual. Cut construction paper into large leaf-shapes. (You'll need about five per person.)

Bring a Peanuts comic strip from the newspaper for each person.

The Session

■ Dig

Have kids each use a piece of paper and a marker, to create a picture of their favorite Peanuts character. Have them tape their pictures on themselves.

Gather the group in a circle. Say: **When I mention the Peanuts comic strip, what's the first thing that comes to your mind?**

After several people have responded, hand out the comic strips you brought. Ask:

● **What can we learn about life by reading Peanuts?**

● **How does Snoopy approach life? Charlie Brown? Lucy?**

● **Who's your favorite character? Why?**

● **What's the difference between an optimistic outlook and a pessimistic outlook? Which do you have most of the time?**

■ Discover

Say: **Ecclesiastes is one of those tough books in the Old Testament. So much of it seems negative. But there's more to this book than you might realize. Let's explore it together.**

Give a "Scripture Dig" handout to each person. Assign each person one or more scriptures from the sheet to research. Ask kids each to decide whether their passage shows a positive, negative or indifferent approach to life. For example, the person with Ecclesiastes 1:2 might say "negative" because the author says life is meaningless.

Place paper, markers and masking tape in the center of the circle. Have everyone share responses. Every time a negative evaluation is given, have the person giving it make a paper airplane and sail it into the air. Every time someone gives a positive evaluation, have that person draw a happy face on a piece of paper and tape it on the wall. Have each person giving an indifferent evaluation wad up a piece of paper and throw it somewhere in the room. When finished with the reports, tally the numbers of responses and see which perspective wins. Ask:

● **What view do you feel the author has toward life?**

● **What might be some reasons for that view?**

● **How do you feel about the author's final conclusion?**
(Read Ecclesiastes 9:7; 12:13-14)

● **Who do you know who views life like this author? What causes that person to view life that way?**

● **In what ways do you share these viewpoints? not share them?**

■ Experience

Say: **When we take a cynical or pessimistic attitude toward life we miss out on God's gifts.**

Draw the group's attention to the tree on the wall. Place the leaves, markers, and masking tape in the center of the room. Say: **The "life tree" on the wall represents your life. The limbs refer to four major areas of life in which God has given us great gifts. On each leaf write a gift that comes to mind. Then tape each leaf to its appropriate limb. For example, a car is a material gift that makes life more enjoyable. A physical gift from God is health or intelligence. Be creative.**

When the tree's completed, survey the various gifts.

Ask:

● **Why do we sometimes forget about all these good things?**

● **Which of the four areas was easiest to find examples for? Explain.**

● **In what ways have you been able to show appreciation for these joys of life?**

■ Grow

Say: **When we feel that life is pointless, it's like falling into a dark hole. Sometimes we see no way out. It's okay to ask the "big" questions, but we also need to realize that not knowing the answers now doesn't mean we never will.**

Ask:

● **When was a time you felt life was pointless?**

● **As a teenager what have been some things you've had a tough time waiting for?**

● **How do you think Jesus felt about his life on Earth?**

● **What gave his life meaning?**

■ Go

Gather everyone in a circle. Ask kids each to pick their favorite Peanuts cartoon character. Hand out paper. On their piece ask kids each to write and complete "I am most like . . . (favorite Peanuts character) when I . . ." When kids are ready, have them share their responses.

Close with this prayer: **Dear God, help us to look for the good in our lives. Help us to seek out ways you're at work. Life is not meaningless. You have a plan for each one of us and we know you'll help us make our lives the best they can possibly be. In Jesus' name, amen.**

Scripture Dig

Instructions: Look up the passage assigned to you and decide whether it shows a positive, negative or indifferent approach to life.

- Ecclesiastes 1:2-11

- Ecclesiastes 2:18-26

- Ecclesiastes 3:1-8

- Ecclesiastes 3:16—4:3

- Ecclesiastes 4:4-16

- Ecclesiastes 5:1-9

- Ecclesiastes 5:10—6:12

- Ecclesiastes 7:1-29

- Ecclesiastes 8:1-15

- Ecclesiastes 8:16—9:12

- Ecclesiastes 9:13—10:20

- Ecclesiastes 11:1-8

- Ecclesiastes 11:9—12:7

- Ecclesiastes 12:8, 13-14

Love Letters

■ Theme: Giving love (Song of Songs)

This short book (also known as Song of Solomon) is a love poem. It describes the ideal of love and courtship. It was probably used as part of the marriage service in Hebrew history. This book reflects the covenant relationship between bridegroom and bride.

Teenagers spend a lot of time thinking about love. The question "How will I know when I'm really in love?" fills the minds of many young people. This session helps kids understand God's perspective on love and sexual relationships within marriage.

■ Objectives

During this session participants will:
- discuss the Song of Songs;
- talk about society's view toward love; and
- write love letters reflecting different kinds of love.

■ Preparation

Read and study the Song of Songs.

Gather Bibles, pencils, paper, markers, a supply of cinnamon candy hearts and glue. Bring one copy of *The Living Bible*.

Collect several advice columns from newspapers. Look for ones dealing with love or relationships.

Make a copy of the "Scripture Dig" handouts for each person.

Cut out 14 large hearts from red construction paper.

Buy or borrow a copy of Peter Cetera's song "Glory of Love" from the *Solitude/Solitaire* album (Full Moon Records). You will also need something to play it on. If you can't obtain this song, find another one about Christian love.

The Session

■ Dig

Gather everyone in a circle and distribute the advice columns. Say: **Read what I just gave you, and decide what attitude the column presents about love.**

Have kids share responses. Then ask each person to complete this statement: "You know you're in love when . . ." Ask:

- **What's the difference between lust and love?**
- **How many times have you truly been in love? How did you know?**
- **What does being in love with someone mean to you?**

■ Discover

Say: **Today we'll explore a small book in the Old Testament that deals entirely with a love relationship between a man and woman. It's a beautiful affirmation of marriage and sexual love.**

Hand out the "Scripture Dig" sheet and assign one or more passages to each group member. With each scripture passage you assign, hand out a red paper heart. Ask kids each to read their passage and write on their heart how they might phrase those verses to someone they love.

Have kids each read their passage and share what they wrote. Read the same passage from *The Living Bible*. When everyone has responded, ask:

- **Why do you think this book is in the Bible?**
- **What does the author want us to know about love?**
- **How has courtship changed since this book was written?**
- **Why is there so much confusion about love these days?**

■ Experience

Say: **There are different kinds of love. Strong feelings between guys and girls grow out of physical love. There's also a love that exists between family members. Another love describes the Christian expression of affection for others. Love has many facets.**

Form five groups. Hand out paper to each group. Have each group write a love letter to one of the following:

- Your future spouse on your wedding day
- Your mother or father
- Your best friend
- Jesus

● A person you're dating and feel you love

Bring the groups together and share the love letters. Ask:

● **What should be included in a love letter?**

● **What was difficult about composing your letter?**

● **Were you worried about what other people might think if you said certain things? Why?**

● **Have you ever received a love letter? What did it do to you?**

● **Have you ever sent a love letter? What did it do for you?**

■ Grow

Say: **We saw at the beginning of this session that society presents confusing pictures of sex and love. But God's perspective keeps sex within the context of marriage.**

Ask:

● **What's the difference between sex and love?**

● **What did God intend sexual love to be like?**

● **Why is it so difficult to wait until marriage for sex?**

● **How many of you want your marriage partner to be a virgin? Does that hold for you as well? Why or why not?**

■ Go

Gather everyone in a circle. Have a volunteer read aloud I Corinthians 13:4-7.

Place the white paper, cinnamon candy hearts and glue in the center of the group. Tell the kids each to make a heart on a sheet of paper by gluing the pieces of candy on the page. Have participants write inside the heart an expression of love to someone special. It might be a friend, a boyfriend or girlfriend, or a parent. Encourage kids each to give their heart to the person they designed it for.

While the group is working, play the song "Glory of Love" by Peter Cetera. When kids have finished making their hearts, compare this song's message to the love of God. Ask each person:

What do you think is "the glory of love"?

Close with this prayer: **Dear God, you've commanded us to love each other. Thank you for your power to love. Thank you for relationships between people that feel good and right. Help us give you control of our relationships. Show us how to love each other better. In Jesus' name, amen.**

Enjoy eating left-over cinnamon candy hearts.

Scripture Dig

Instructions: Rewrite your assigned passage as though writing to someone you love.

- Song of Songs 1:2-4

- Song of Songs 1:5-6

- Song of Songs 1:7-8

- Song of Songs 1:9—2:7

- Song of Songs 2:8-17

- Song of Songs 3:1-5

- Song of Songs 3:6-11

- Song of Songs 4:1-7

- Song of Songs 4:8-15

- Song of Songs 5:2-8, 10-16

- Song of Songs 6:4-12

- Song of Songs 7:1-9

- Song of Songs 8:1-4

- Song of Songs 8:5b-7

Crime and Punishment

■ Theme: Suffering the consequences (Isaiah)

Isaiah stood in awe of God's power. He repeatedly referred to the "Holy One of Israel" and tried to draw Judah back under the umbrella of God's will. He challenged the people of Judah to put aside the evil in the land so that God wouldn't reject them. Yet he also offered hope for restoration.

The book of Isaiah contains two parts. This session explores both parts, dealing with examples of God's warnings in chapter 1, and God's encouragement to the remnant in chapters 40 and 41. This session helps kids see the ultimate consequences of their actions.

■ Objectives

During this session participants will:
- study themes from Isaiah;
- identify the relationship between action and consequence;
- create sculptures that depict the consequences of various actions; and
- discuss the way God's justice works in the world.

■ Preparation

Scan the book of Isaiah.

Gather paper, markers, pencils, a coin and Bibles. Buy a prize for the winning team in the Discover section.

Draw various traffic signs on separate pieces of 8 1/2 × 11 paper. Make one sign for each person, and hang the signs around the room.

Make enough copies of the "Sticky Situations" for each person to have one strip.

Bring enough modeling clay (Play-Doh brand works best) for each participant to have a golf-ball-size piece.

The Session

∎ Dig

Say: **Today we're going to take a driver's test. Hanging around the room are a variety of traffic signs. As I point to each sign tell me what it stands for and what would happen if I didn't obey it.**

After the test, hand out pieces of paper and markers. Ask each person to pick one sign and write a caption for it that might apply to a life situation. For example, a caption for a "curve" sign might read, "If you don't change your actions you'll end up wrecking your life."

Have the kids share their captions. Then ask:

● **What kinds of people in our society do you think fail to consider the consequences of their actions?**

● **Why do people often not think about consequences?**

∎ Discover

Say: **The prophet Isaiah was called by God to try to bring the people of Judah back to their spiritual roots to avert disaster. The book's first 39 chapters deal with Isaiah's struggles with Judah. Chapters 40 to 66 offer encouragement for Judah after the nation suffered the consequences of their actions when they went into exile.**

Divide the group into two teams. Seat the teams so they face each other. Ask each team to decide on a "family" team name, such as "the Bradys" or "the Huxtables."

Give paper and a pencil to each team. Assign one team Isaiah 1:1-20. Assign the other team Isaiah 40:1-11 and Isaiah 41:17-20. Have the teams study all three passages. Instruct each team to write 10 questions about the other team's scripture. After both teams have written their questions, flip a coin to see which team asks its 10 questions first. Allow the teams 30 seconds to answer each question (they may not use their Bibles). Every correct answer counts 100 points. Give a prize to the winning team.

Bring the groups together and ask:

● **What brought God's judgment on the people?**

● **Why wouldn't the people listen to Isaiah's warnings?**

● **Why did God reach out to the people in exile?**

∎ Experience

Say: **The prophet Isaiah warned the people of Judah about the consequences of their actions. Judah didn't listen and Isaiah's predictions came true. Let's look at some situations we**

might face and how our actions might determine the consequences.

Distribute the "Sticky Situations" strips you cut earlier and the golf-ball-size pieces of clay. Have kids each read their situation and sculpt their clay to represent the most likely consequence of the action described. Tell kids they can sculpt their clay to represent a physical consequence, such as a broken leg, or an emotional or spiritual consequence, such as depression or a bad attitude toward God.

When everyone has finished, have kids each share their situation and explain their clay sculpture. Ask the group to think of other possible consequences.

After everyone has shared, ask:

● **What are the consequences of going against God's will?**

● **When have your actions resulted in a consequence you didn't expect?**

● **Do you think it's fair for every bad deed to have a bad consequence? What if we regret the action afterward and never do it again?**

Read aloud Matthew 5:44-45. Then ask:

● **Does God sometimes let people "get by" without suffering the consequences of their actions? Explain.**

■ Grow

Say: **In every age, some people seem to never face the consequences of their actions: a criminal who's never caught, a schoolmate who avoids punishment for wrong actions, a rich person who never pays taxes. At the same time, some people who do admirable deeds never get any recognition for their actions. At times we may feel that God isn't fair.**

Have a volunteer read aloud Psalm 73:2-13. Then ask:

● **When was a time you felt someone didn't get what they deserved?**

● **When was a time you felt you didn't get what you deserved?**

● **How do you explain why some "wicked" people never get caught?**

Say: **Now let's hear the rest of the Psalm to see the writer's conclusion about the "prosperity of the wicked."**

Have another volunteer read aloud Psalm 73:16-20. Then ask:

● **What does the phrase "you reap what you sow" mean to you?**

● **How does the phrase apply to people who seem to avoid the consequences of their actions?**

● **From our discussion, do you think God is just? Why or why not?**

■ Go

Gather everyone in a circle. Take down the traffic signs and give one to each participant. Ask kids each to write on their sign one wrong action God has allowed them to do without facing the consequences. Encourage kids to repent of that action and turn their lives over to God. Ask kids each to hang their sign in their bedroom as a reminder of their decision.

Close with this prayer: **Dear God, help us look to you for direction. Help us consider the consequences of our actions, both for ourselves and those around us. And teach us to make wise choices. Thank you for your mercy. In Jesus' name, amen.**

Sticky Situations

Instructions: Cut these situations into strips. Make enough copies so that each participant can have one strip.

✂ --

- You jump off a cliff.

- You yell at your parents because you're in a bad mood.

- You cheat on a test.

- You talk behind someone's back.

- You have sex with your girlfriend/boyfriend.

- You don't study for a test.

- You start smoking.

- You start using drugs.

- You start hanging around with the wrong crowd.

- You sneak out of the house to go to a bar.

- You break the speed limit.

- You stop spending time alone with God.

Standing Alone

■ Theme: Facing persecution (Jeremiah)

Jeremiah's prophecy came during Judah's declining years. After King Josiah's death, Jeremiah repeatedly called the people back to God. But corrupt, evil kings walked the nation into disaster. Jeremiah's words brought him ridicule. The people despised his presence. Jeremiah shared his agony of loneliness through the pages of his writings.

Persecution comes in many forms. Jeremiah faced it because he dared to stand up for God.

Teenagers face persecution for the same reason and sometimes wonder if faith or moral character is worth the ridicule. This session helps teenagers share their feelings about persecution and encourages them to give God control of their lives—whatever the cost.

■ Objectives

During this session participants will:
- explore themes in Jeremiah;
- take a poll about how much persecution they'd endure;
- identify times when they've faced persecution; and
- covenant to be willing to receive persecution for God.

■ Preparation

Scan the book of Jeremiah.

Gather Bibles, a tennis ball, masking tape and several red markers.

Make a copy of the "Scripture Dig" handout for each person.

Prepare a short talk on Abraham Lincoln's career, but don't reveal who you're talking about until the end of your talk. Emphasize the times he faced persecution and failure, yet didn't give in. Refer to this brief overview. Over a 30-year period, this man:
- lost his business;
- lost in a race for state representative;
- lost his business again;
- lost his sweetheart;
- had a nervous breakdown;
- lost a bid for speaker of the House of Representatives;
- lost a race for elector;

● lost two races for U.S. representative;
● lost a race for U.S. senator;
● lost a race for Vice-President of the United States; and
● lost a race for U.S. senator.

On a sheet of newsprint draw an outline of a large cross. Across the top write "Covenant Cross." Have the cross ready to tape on the wall.

The Session

■ Dig

Say: **Today we're going to discuss persecution. Persecution can be anything from someone giving you a dirty look to brutally murdering you—for who you are or what you stand for. Let's look first at whether you'd be willing to face persecution for your beliefs.**

Ask kids to respond to the following statements by:
● standing—if they would *definitely* risk facing persecution;
● staying seated—if they *might* risk facing persecution; or
● covering their eyes—if they *wouldn't* risk facing persecution.

Read these statements, one at a time.
I would risk facing persecution to . . .
● **protect a close friend.**
● **stand up for what I believe.**
● **disagree with my parents.**
● **disagree with my peer group.**
● **stand up for my personal honor.**
● **fight for the rights of the poor.**
● **speak out on racial intolerance at my school.**
● **listen to certain music.**
● **associate with people my friends don't like.**
● **choose the college my parents don't like.**
● **turn down a drink.**
● **abstain from sex.**

■ Discover

Have kids stand in a circle. Say: **Jeremiah was a great prophet. But the people of Judah didn't like him. They beat him, threw him in jail, ridiculed him and made it quite clear he wasn't welcome. He endured, but his writings reveal the pain he felt—the same kind of pain we feel when others persecute us for our beliefs.**

Distribute the "Scripture Dig" handouts and Bibles. Bounce the tennis ball to someone in the circle. Have him or her read aloud the first passage from the "Scripture Dig" handout. Then have that person bounce the ball to someone else in the circle. Have the second person read the second passage from the handout. Continue until all the verses have been read.

Discuss the passages and Jeremiah's life. Then ask:

- **What bothered Jeremiah about the people's behavior?**
- **What kind of loneliness was he feeling?**
- **Why did the people dislike him so much?**
- **If you had been Jeremiah, how would you have handled the rejection and persecution?**

■ Experience

Give your talk about Abraham Lincoln's life, but don't reveal who you're talking about or that he eventually became President. After explaining Lincoln's history, ask:

Who do you think I'm talking about?

After kids offer ideas, say: **In 1860, after this 30-year struggle, this man was elected President of the United States—Abraham Lincoln.**

Discuss the way Lincoln faced rejection and failure but still kept coming back until he became President.

Tell the group you're going to read aloud three open-ended statements. After you read the first statement, have kids pair up. Have the partners each tell the other how they'd complete the statement. Read the next statement, then have kids find new partners and share their responses to that statement. Do the same for the third statement.

Read these statements:

- **The greatest rejection I ever faced in a relationship was when . . .**
- **The worst persecution I ever faced at school was because of . . .**
- **The most memorable time I ever stood up for God was . . .**

Bring everyone together and have kids discuss what they shared.

■ Grow

Say: **Enduring persecution for God is tough. Yet there are times when you have to stand up—like Jeremiah—and be counted for your beliefs.**

Ask:

- **What qualities do you see in Jeremiah that you would like to have?**
- **How is faith strengthened by persecution?**
- **Would you rather live during a time of heavy persecu-**

tion or light persecution? Explain.
● **What in your life would you be willing to fight to keep?**

■ Covenant

Tape the "Covenant Cross" on the wall. Place several red markers near the cross. Gather everyone in a half-circle around it. Read aloud Matthew 5:10-12. Then say: **Tonight I agree to risk facing persecution for the Lord.**

Walk to the cross and sign your name with a red marker. Then return to your place. Stand quietly and say nothing. Wait for others to follow your example.

■ Go

Close by singing together "I Have Decided to Follow Jesus" from *Songs* (Songs & Creations).

Scripture Dig

Instructions: Be prepared to read the next passage if the ball is bounced to you.

- Jeremiah 1:4-10

- Jeremiah 2:1-2, 20-22

- Jeremiah 4:5-8

- Jeremiah 6:19, 22-23

- Jeremiah 7:2-8

- Jeremiah 11:18—12:6

- Jeremiah 13:1-11

- Jeremiah 15:15-21

- Jeremiah 18:1-12

- Jeremiah 20:1-6

- Jeremiah 30:18-22

- Jeremiah 31:31-34

All the Losers Win

■ Theme: Becoming a winner (Ezekiel)

Ezekiel was carried off with King Jehoiachin in the initial Babylonian attack in 597 B.C. He prophesied during the years before Jerusalem's destruction and after Judah's exile.

In his book, Ezekiel shares many visions from God and unique experiences. One of the best-known experiences occurred in the "valley of dry bones." God used this experience to encourage Ezekiel and to reveal God's power to restore Israel to its former glory.

Teenagers often live with disappointments and hurts that cause them to lose hope in themselves and their world. This session helps kids bring those hurts out in the open so God can begin restoring their lives to what he intended them to be.

■ Objectives

During this session participants will:
● research the "valley of dry bones" scene from Ezekiel;
● do a simulation game involving pretend injuries;
● explore how God can use them to help heal others' hurts; and
● have the opportunity to open their hurts to God and a friend.

■ Preparation

Scan the book of Ezekiel. Read and study Ezekiel 37:1-14.

Make enough copies of the "Injury Strips" handout so that each person is assigned an injury.

Gather Bibles and a package of red and a package of yellow stickers.

Cut out red construction paper hearts (about 4 inches wide). Staple two hearts together along one side to make a heart-card. Make a heart-card for each person.

For "Shadow Crosses," you'll need a table, a cross (8 to 12 inches high), three short candles and matches. You'll also need candleholders and a base for the cross. Set the cross and candles on the table about 1 foot away from a wall. Refer to the diagram on page 158. When the lights are off, the lit candles and single cross should project an image of three crosses on the wall. (Try this before the session to be sure it's set up correctly.)

Buy or borrow a recording of "He's All You Need" from Steve Camp's *One on One* album (Sparrow). You'll also need something to play it on. If you can't obtain this song, find another one on God's faithfulness.

The Session

■ Dig

Say: **We're going to start with a simulation exercise. I have several strips of paper that each describe a different physical injury. In a moment, we're going to go outside and I'm going to give each of you one of the strips. Each of you will role-play the injury listed on your strip. For instance, if your strip says "Your left leg is broken," role-play that by hopping around on your right leg. Your goal in this exercise is to get back to the meeting room.**

Take the group outside and distribute the paper strips. Tell the kids to stay in character until everyone is back in the meeting room.

When everyone is back inside, ask:

● **What was difficult about this exercise?**

● **How did it feel for those of you with serious injuries? What was your attitude toward those with less serious injuries?**

● **How did those of you with less serious injuries feel about the more seriously injured people? Did you help them back to the meeting room? Why or why not?**

■ Discover

Say: **Our scriptures today explore the prophet Ezekiel's life. Ezekiel was carried into exile when Babylon conquered Judah. Ten years later Babylon wrecked Jerusalem and destroyed the temple. Ezekiel served as God's spokesman, encouraging the people to repent of their sinful ways. On many occasions, God spoke to Ezekiel through visions and dreams. One of the most famous examples is the "valley of dry bones" scene in Ezekiel 37.**

Form five groups, and assign each group one of these passages to summarize for the whole group:

● Ezekiel 37:1-3
● Ezekiel 37:4-6
● Ezekiel 37:7-8
● Ezekiel 37:9-10
● Ezekiel 37:11-14

Hand kids each a sheet of red stickers and a sheet of yellow stickers. Tell them the yellow stickers represent hope and the red stickers represent doom. As each group explains each of its verses to the whole group, have the presenting group place one yellow or red sticker (depending on whether the verse conveys hope or doom) on each person in the other groups. When the groups finish, decide which color is most prominent.

Ask:

- **How did Ezekiel use the image of the bones?**
- **Do you ever feel "dried up"—like bones in a desert?**
Explain.
- **How does God's action on the dry bones apply to you?**
- **What does this story tell you about God?**

■ Experience

Gather everyone in a semicircle. Distribute a heart-card and a pencil to each person. Say: **Think about the most painful problem you're facing. It may be a rough family situation, poor self-esteem or a problem you're having with someone close to you. Write that problem inside your heart. Write your name on the outside of the heart. Later, you'll share with one other person what you wrote in your card.**

While kids are writing, light the three candles in front of the cross (refer to the diagram below).

After the kids have finished writing, say: **I'm going to turn the lights off and play a song. While the song plays, concentrate on the "Shadow Crosses." Talk to God about your problem. Give your problem to God and let him begin to heal your hurt.**

Turn the lights off and play the song "He's All You Need" by Steve Camp. Leave the lights off awhile after the song finishes.

Say: **Many of you have just given your problem to God. Now he can begin to turn your "dry bones" into an "army" for his glory. If you've given your problem to God, place your heart on the floor beneath the Shadow Crosses.**

After kids have laid their hearts on the floor, turn the lights on.

■ Grow

Ask:

● **How did you feel about writing your greatest problem on the heart?**

● **Why is it hard to give problems to God?**

● **What does it mean to give problems to God?**

Read aloud Galatians 6:2. Then say: **It's hard to carry burdens alone. Sometimes we're afraid that other people will reject us if they know about our problems. But the Bible commands us to share our burdens with other Christians. I'm going to ask you to do something that will require you to risk being vulnerable with another person. Find the person who is most directly across from you. Quietly get your heart from the pile and give it to that person. Then return to your seat.** (Be ready to participate in this activity yourself.)

After kids have returned to their seats, ask:

● **How did it feel when you gave your heart to someone else?**

● **How did it feel to receive a heart from someone else?**

● **How do you think God feels when we share our burdens with him?**

● **What should you do with the knowledge you received in the heart?**

■ Go

Have kids each go to the person who gave them a heart and pray about the person's problem. Encourage kids each to become an ongoing prayer partner with another group member.

Dismiss kids after they finish praying together.

Injury Strips

Instructions: Cut the following conditions into strips. Photocopy the list if necessary so that everyone gets a strip.

- Your left leg is broken.

- You're unconscious.

- You're paralyzed from the waist down.

- You're blind.

- Both of your arms are broken.

- You're blind and can't speak.

- Your right arm is broken.

The Man Who Wouldn't Stop Praying

■ Theme: Facing trials (Daniel)

The book of Daniel affirms the truth that God is sovereign—over individuals and nations. Daniel records God's miraculous intervention in faithful lives, which in turn had astonishing effects on non-believers. Chapters 1 to 6 relate those stories, and chapters 7 to 12 contain Daniel's writing concerning future things. This session focuses on the stories of Daniel and his three friends: Hananiah, Mishael and Azariah (better known as Shadrach, Meshach and Abednego).

Teenagers experience many trials. They experience "lion's den" moments when they feel they're being devoured. They often walk into a "blazing furnace" of problems and stress. This session helps kids see a purpose in those trials.

■ Objectives

During this session participants will:
● review the stories in Daniel 1—6;
● talk about what it's like to be on the "hot seat";
● identify "lion's den" and "furnace" trials in life; and
● discuss ways to respond to trials effectively.

■ Preparation

Read and study Daniel 1—6.

Gather Bibles, paper and pencils.

On one sheet of red construction paper, write "Hot Seat." Then tape it to the back of a chair.

On a chalkboard, write the following references:
● Daniel 1:1-21
● Daniel 2:1-49
● Daniel 3:1-30
● Daniel 5:1-31
● Daniel 6:1-28

The Session

■ Dig

Gather everyone in a circle and set the "hot seat" chair in the center. Ask kids to think about their responses to this statement: "I feel like I'm on the hot seat when . . ."

One at a time, have each person sit in the chair and give one response to the statement. For example, "I feel like I'm on the hot seat when a teacher criticizes my work in class."

Repeat the process, but ask kids to complete: "I put others on the hot seat when I . . ." For example, "I put others on the hot seat when I drive too fast, and they're in the car with me."

Ask:
- **What do you sometimes feel like doing when you go through "hot seat" trials?**
- **How do you try to get yourself out of trials?**
- **What kind of trials are you going through?**

■ Discover

Say: **Today we'll explore the book of Daniel. Some of you may remember this book's stories from your childhood.**

Form five groups (a group can be one person) and assign each group one of the references you wrote on the chalkboard earlier. Ask each group to prepare to explain the verses to the whole group and to share how its members might've felt in Daniel's place.

When groups are prepared, bring them together and have them share their responses. Then ask:
- **What do you admire about Daniel's faith?**
- **Why wasn't Daniel willing to stop his daily prayers?**
- **What would you have done in Daniel's place?**
- **How do these stories help us understand the ways God rewards obedience?**

■ Experience

Divide the group into two. Give each group paper and pencils. Have one group be the "furnace" people and the other group be the "lion's den" people.

Say: **In your group, list all the ways you feel you've experienced being thrown in the "furnace" or the "lion's den." Be specific. Also, list ways you feel you've put others in those places.**

Pick two rooms in your church that might correspond most closely to the two groups. Send the "furnace" group to the boiler/furnace room to do its work. Send the "lion's den" group to your church's basement area (or a similar room). Give each group 10 minutes to complete its tasks. Send an adult volunteer with each group to make sure it stays on track.

Bring the groups together and share insights.

■ Grow

Say: **We all go through furnace and lion's den experiences. We face them at school, at home and with friends. We sometimes wonder if God is with us during those times when everything seems against us.**

Ask:

● **What do these stories from Daniel tell us about faith in God?**

● **How do we try to protect ourselves from trials?**

● **Of these groups—friends, parents or teachers—who do you feel throws you to the lions the most? Explain.**

● **Why do we have to experience trials like these?**

■ Go

Gather everyone in a circle. Place the "hot seat" in the center of the group again. Ask kids to complete: "When I face trials I need to ask God . . ." Have each person sit in the "hot seat" and share a response. For example, "When I face trials, I need to ask God to help me have patience with the situation."

Read aloud James 1:2-4. Close with this prayer: **Dear God, every day we find ourselves in the "furnace." Someone gets mad at us. Someone puts us down. Someone uses us as emotional punching bags. The trials we face can really get us down. Strengthen us by your Holy Spirit to endure those tough times. Give us wisdom to know when we're treating others wrongly. In Jesus' name, amen.**

When You Don't Get What You Deserve

■ Theme: Receiving mercy (Jonah)

Nineveh was immersed in idolatry. To the Jews, the hated Ninevites represented the ultimate evil and contempt for God's rule. No wonder Jonah had a hard time understanding God's call for him to show mercy to those Jonah hated so much.

In the book of Jonah we find people who repented when confronted with God's judgment. The Hebrews, however, refused to acknowledge that they too faced God's judgment if they didn't return to God.

Mercy is a vital part of our relationship to God. This session helps kids understand and appreciate the magnitude of God's mercy.

■ Objectives

During this session participants will:
● read the book of Jonah;
● identify spiritual insights contained in Jonah;
● share an experience of feeling shut-off from God; and
● discuss ways they have experienced God's mercy.

■ Preparation

Read and study the book of Jonah.

Gather markers, masking tape, candles, matches and Bibles.

On a sheet of newsprint write "Mercy is . . ." and tape it on the wall. Look up the dictionary definition of mercy.

Outline a large fish on a sheet of newsprint and tape it on the wall. Across the top of the newsprint write, "A time this week when I experienced mercy was . . ."

Make a copy of "Fishy Verses" for each person. Also make enough copies of the "Fish Shape" page so each person can have three "fish."

Locate a small, windowless room where you can take the group. Memorize the questions in the Experience section.

The Session

■ Dig

Distribute markers and ask kids to write phrases to complete "Mercy is . . ." on the newsprint. While they're writing, place the blank fish shapes and masking tape in the center of the room. As kids finish their definitions, have them respond to "A time this week when I experienced mercy was . . ." by writing their responses on fish shapes and taping them inside the large fish outline on the wall. For example, a person might write "A time this week when I experienced mercy was when I came into math class late and the teacher didn't yell at me about it."

When everyone has finished, have kids share their responses.

■ Discover

Say: **Today we explore the book of Jonah. What do you remember about Jonah? Let's read his story together.**

Hand out the "Fishy Verses" and let each person read his or her passage to the group.

Ask:

- **Why did Jonah get angry with God?**
- **What point does God try to make with Jonah?**
- **What in Jonah's life is similar to your experiences?**

■ Experience

Hand each person a candle and keep one yourself. Take kids to the windowless room you picked out. Take matches and a Bible. Leave the lights off and close the door behind you.

Ask (from memory):

- **What would it be like to stay three days in the awful darkness and stench inside a big fish?**
- **What might the fish in the book of Jonah symbolize?**
- **When was a time when you felt shut-off, isolated from God?**
- **What did you do to escape from the darkness of that moment?**
- **Who do you know who's caught in that kind of darkness? How could you help?**

Light the candle you're holding. Say: **This candle symbolizes God's mercy. Listen again to these words of Jonah as he cries out to God.** (Read aloud Jonah 2:1-10.) **Now listen to these words from John.** (Read aloud John 1:1-5.)

Light one other person's candle as you say: **I'm going to pass** the light to one of you, and I want you to light each other's candles. God's mercy is like this light. Even when we feel trapped in darkness, God's mercy takes hold of us. God's mercy is the candle that brings blessing where judgment is deserved.

Enjoy the brightness of the candlelight for a couple of minutes, then have kids blow out their candles and return to the meeting room.

■ Grow

Gather kids in a circle. Read the dictionary definition of mercy. Ask:

- Do most people in our country believe in the concept of mercy? Why or why not?
- Why does God often choose to bless us even though we deserve punishment?
- Do you usually show mercy toward others, or do you like to see people get what they deserve?
- How can you begin to show more mercy toward others?

■ Go

Have kids each share one way God has shown them mercy. Then read aloud in unison Psalm 103:2-18 as a closing prayer.

Fishy Verses

Instructions: Cut apart each of these fish-shape verses to distribute to the group.

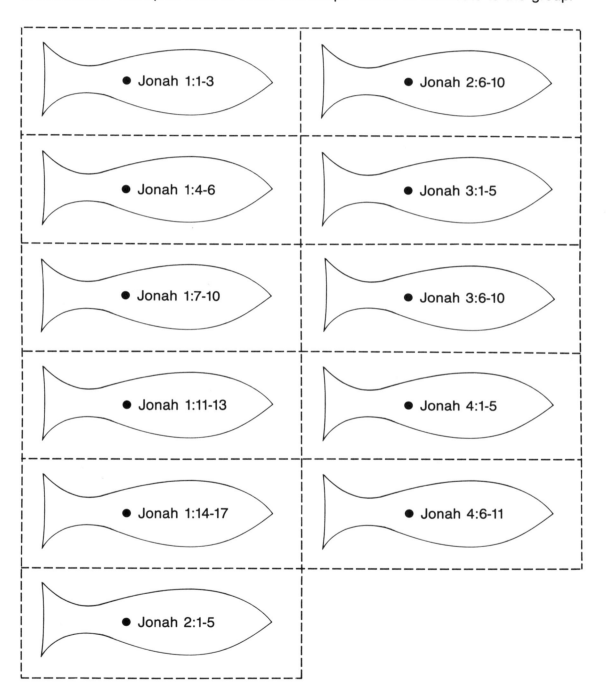

● Jonah 1:1-3

● Jonah 2:6-10

● Jonah 1:4-6

● Jonah 3:1-5

● Jonah 1:7-10

● Jonah 3:6-10

● Jonah 1:11-13

● Jonah 4:1-5

● Jonah 1:14-17

● Jonah 4:6-11

● Jonah 2:1-5

Fish Shape

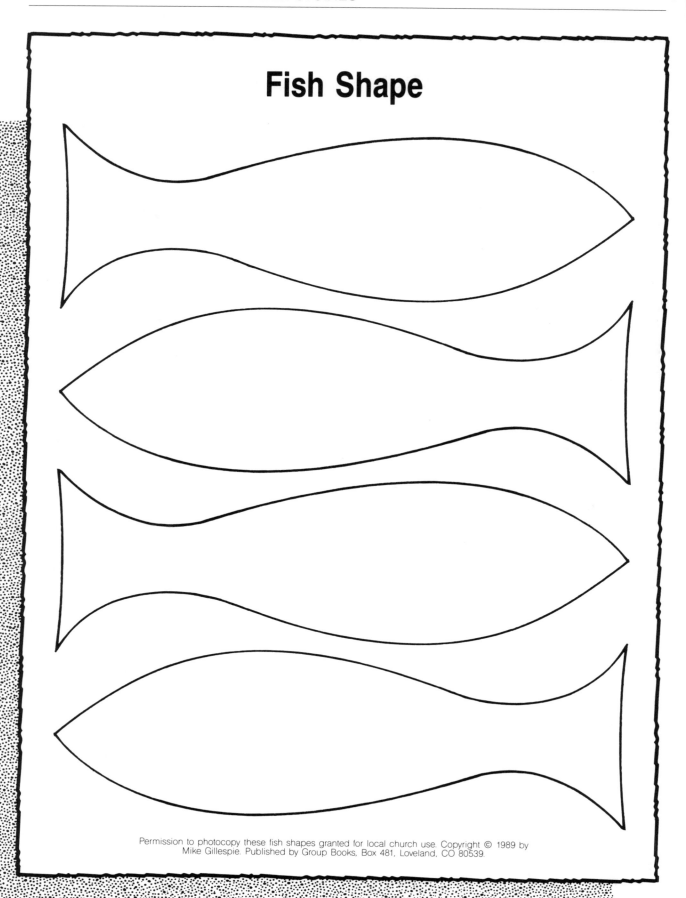

What Does the Lord Require?

■ Theme: Showing kindness (Micah)

Micah made his case against Israel and Judah by picturing a court hearing in which God gave his complaint against the people. Because of their faithless lifestyles, God would exact judgment upon both Israel and Judah. However, Micah promised hope and blessing if the people would return to God.

This session explores mercy as pictured in the famous saying from Micah 6:8. Micah knew one of God's chief requirements was being kind to one another.

Many teenagers are starved for kindness and aren't sure how to show kindness to others without appearing "soft." This session helps kids learn how to demonstrate kindness to others.

■ Objectives

During this session participants will:
● explore the themes from the book of Micah;
● relate common objects to kindness;
● design stained-glass windows that represent acts of kindness; and
● commit to show kindness to someone during the week.

■ Preparation

Read and study the book of Micah.

Gather a package of 3×5 cards, Bibles, pencils, markers, tissue paper, glue, scissors, construction paper and masking tape.

You'll also need an assortment of items kids can keep such as: pencil, balloon, apple, soft drink, happy-face sign, movie ticket, the words "I'm sorry" written on paper, a McDonald's gift certificate, a comic strip or soap. (Add more items of your choice until you have enough for everyone.) Place the objects in a paper sack.

Make enough copies of the "Scripture Cards" for each person to have one card.

The Session

■ Dig

Gather everyone in a circle. Say: **Inside this paper sack are all kinds of items. I'm going to let you stick your hand inside and pull out an item.**

Go around and let kids each pick an item out of the sack. Don't let them look before they pick. Have them each keep their objects for later. Say: **Think for a moment of how the object you hold could be used in an act of kindness to someone. For example, the pencil could be used to write an encouraging note to someone. The movie ticket could be used to take a friend out for a special time.**

Have kids share their responses. Then ask:
- **What's the kindest thing someone did for you last week?**
- **What's the kindest thing you did for someone else?**
- **What feelings do you have when you receive a kindness?**

■ Discover

Say: **Today we're studying the prophet Micah. He was called as a prophet to tell both Israel and Judah they had strayed from God's calling. Let's explore his message.**

Hand each person one blank 3×5 card, one scripture card with a question on it, and a pencil. Have kids each look up their scripture and write the answer to their question on the blank card. Tell them not to include the scripture reference on the answer card.

Take up all the cards. Give each person a new scripture card and answer card. Ask kids each to read their scripture card aloud. Then ask whoever thinks he or she has the right answer card to read it aloud. Keep going until all the questions have been answered correctly.

Ask:
- **What bothered Micah the most?**
- **Does our society commit any of the sins Micah described? Which ones?**
- **Which of these three is the most difficult for you: humility, kindness (mercy), or justice? Explain.**
- **Which one of these three should Christians be most concerned about? Why?**

■ Experience

Pile markers, tissue paper, glue, scissors, construction paper and masking tape in the center of the room. Form five groups. Assign each of the groups one of the following categories:

- Kindness in my family
- Kindness at school
- Kindness in my youth group
- Kindness to people in the world
- Kindness to God

Say: **In each of your groups design a "Kindness Stained-Glass Window" that contains symbols of kindness that apply to your category. For example, for "kindness in my youth group" you might show an ear to represent listening. You can draw the symbols on sheets of tissue paper and then make frames for them out of the construction paper. Don't use words, just symbols.**

(The groups can make one window with many symbols or several different windows, each with one symbol.)

When the groups have finished, let them share the symbolism of their windows. Hang the windows in the meeting area.

■ Grow

Say: **Micah had a tough time trying to rally the people back to God. In fact, Israel eventually fell to the Assyrians. Judah later suffered the same fate at the hands of the Babylonians. Micah's message from God hadn't sunk in.**

Ask:

- **Why is it sometimes hard to show kindness?**
- **Who can you show kindness to most easily? Why?**
- **How would life be different if we eliminated all acts of kindness?**
- **What does it mean to "walk humbly with your God"?**
- **When kindness, justice and humility are not important in a society, where will that society end up?**

■ Go

Gather everyone in a circle. Have kids each get the objects they selected at the start of the session. Ask kids each what act of kindness *they* could do with their object in the coming week. Tell them to keep the objects and follow through on their kindnesses.

Share this prayer: **Dear God, the gift of Jesus was the greatest kindness we'll ever know. And there are so many ways we can share kindness each day. Help us reach out to others this week and share Christ's kindness. In Jesus' name, amen.**

Scripture Cards

Instructions: Cut apart each of the following questions. Make enough copies so that each person can have one card.

● What word comes to Micah (Micah 1:1)? Who's in power?	● What's God planning to do (Micah 1:2-4)?	● What will happen to Samaria (Micah 1:6-7)?
● What's going to fall on Judah (Micah 1:8-9)?	● What are the sins of the people (Micah 2:1-2)?	● What's God going to do about the people's sins (Micah 2:3-11)?
● What hope is held out (Micah 2:12-13)?	● How are the people exploited (Micah 3:1-4)?	● How is the nation impoverished (Micah 3:9-12)?
● What image is painted of the future (Micah 4:1-5)?	● How will God reign over the people (Micah 4:6-13)?	● Who's coming (Micah 5:2-15)?
● What are complaints God has against the people (Micah 6:1-16)?	● What will be Israel's final hope in captivity (Micah 7:8-13)?	

Index of Topics

The Old Testament isn't just history. It deals with today's issues. Use this topical index to pinpoint your young people's concerns. Then use the sessions best suited to meet their needs.

MORE INNOVATIVE RESOURCES FOR YOUR YOUTH MINISTRY

The Youth Worker's Encyclopedia of Bible-Teaching Ideas: Old Testament/ New Testament

Explore the most comprehensive idea-books available for youth workers! Discover more than 350 creative ideas in each of these 400-page encyclopedias—there's at least one idea for each and every book of the Bible. Find ideas for...retreats and overnighters, learning games, adventures, special projects, parties, prayers, music, devotions, skits, and much more!

Plus, you can use these ideas for groups of all sizes in any setting. Large or small. Sunday or mid-week meeting. Bible study. Sunday school class or retreat. Discover exciting new ways to teach each book of the Bible to your youth group.

Old Testament   ISBN 1-55945-184-X
New Testament   ISBN 1-55945-183-1

Clip-Art Cartoons for Churches

Here are over 180 funny, photocopiable illustrations to help you jazz up your calendars, newsletters, posters, fliers, transparencies, postcards, business cards, announcements—all your printed materials! These fun, fresh illustrations cover a variety of church and Christian themes, including church life, Sunday school, youth groups, school life, sermons, church events, volunteers, and more! And there's a variety of artistic styles to choose from so each piece you create will be unique and original.

Each illustration is provided in three different sizes so it's easy to use. You won't find random images here...each image is a complete cartoon. And these cartoons are fun! In fact, they're so entertaining that you may just find yourself reading the book and not photocopying them at all.

Order your copy of **Clip-Art Cartoons for Churches** today...and add some spice to your next printed piece.

ISBN 1-55945-791-0

Bore No More! (For Every Pastor, Speaker, Teacher)

This book is a must for every pastor, youth leader, teacher, and speaker. These 70 audience-grabbing activities pull listeners into your lesson or sermon—and drive your message home!

Discover clever object lessons, creative skits, and readings. Music and celebration ideas. Affirmation activities. All the innovative techniques 85 percent of adult church-goers say they wish their pastors would try! (recent Group Publishing poll)

Involve your congregation in the learning process! These complete 5- to 15-minute activities highlight common New Testament Lectionary passages, so you'll use this book week after week.

ISBN 1-55945-266-8

Order today from your local Christian bookstore, or write: Group Publishing, P.O. Box 485, Loveland, CO 80539.

CURRICULUM REORDER—TOP PRIORITY

Order now to prepare for your upcoming Sunday school classes, youth ministry meetings, and weekend retreats! Each book includes all teacher and student materials—plus photocopiable handouts—for any size class!

FOR JUNIOR HIGH/MIDDLE SCHOOL:

Accepting Others: Beyond Barriers & Stereotypes
ISBN 1-55945-126-2

Advice to Young Christians: Exploring Paul's Letters
ISBN 1-55945-146-7

Applying the Bible to Life, ISBN 1-55945-116-5

Becoming Responsible, ISBN 1-55945-109-2

Bible Heroes: Joseph, Esther, Mary & Peter
ISBN 1-55945-137-8

Boosting Self-Esteem, ISBN 1-55945-100-9

Building Better Friendships, ISBN 1-55945-138-6

Can Christians Have Fun?, ISBN 1-55945-134-3

Caring for God's Creation, ISBN 1-55945-121-1

Christmas: A Fresh Look, ISBN 1-55945-124-6

Dealing With Death, ISBN 1-55945-112-2

Dealing With Disappointment, ISBN 1-55945-139-4

Doing Your Best, ISBN 1-55945-142-4

Drugs & Drinking, ISBN 1-55945-118-1

Evil and the Occult, ISBN 1-55945-102-5

Genesis: The Beginnings, ISBN 1-55945-111-4

Guys & Girls: Understanding Each Other
ISBN 1-55945-110-6

Handling Conflict, ISBN 1-55945-125-4

Heaven & Hell, ISBN 1-55945-131-9

Is God Unfair?, ISBN 1-55945-108-4

Love or Infatuation?, ISBN 1-55945-128-9

Making Parents Proud, ISBN 1-55945-107-6

Materialism, ISBN 1-55945-130-0

The Miracle of Easter, ISBN 1-55945-143-2

Miracles!, ISBN 1-55945-117-3

Peace & War, ISBN 1-55945-123-8

Peer Pressure, ISBN 1-55945-103-3

Prayer, ISBN 1-55945-104-1

Reaching Out to a Hurting World, ISBN 1-55945-140-8

Sermon on the Mount, ISBN 1-55945-129-7

Suicide: The Silent Epidemic, ISBN 1-55945-145-9

Telling Your Friends About Christ, ISBN 1-55945-114-9

The Ten Commandments, ISBN 1-55945-127-0

Today's Faith Heroes, ISBN 1-55945-141-6

Today's Media: Choosing Wisely, ISBN 1-55945-144-0

Today's Music: Good or Bad?, ISBN 1-55945-101-7

What Is God's Purpose for Me?, ISBN 1-55945-132-7

What's a Christian?, ISBN 1-55945-105-X

FOR SENIOR HIGH:

1 & 2 Corinthians: Christian Discipleship
ISBN 1-55945-230-7

Angels, Demons, Miracles & Prayer, ISBN 1-55945-235-8

Changing the World, ISBN 1-55945-236-6

Christians in a Non-Christian World
ISBN 1-55945-224-2

Christlike Leadership, ISBN 1-55945-231-5

Communicating With Friends, ISBN 1-55945-228-5

Counterfeit Religions, ISBN 1-55945-207-2

Dating Decisions, ISBN 1-55945-215-3

Dealing With Life's Pressures, ISBN 1-55945-232-3

Deciphering Jesus' Parables, ISBN 1-55945-237-4

Exodus: Following God, ISBN 1-55945-226-9

Exploring Ethical Issues, ISBN 1-55945-225-0

Faith for Tough Times, ISBN 1-55945-216-1

Forgiveness, ISBN 1-55945-223-4

Getting Along With Parents, ISBN 1-55945-202-1

Getting Along With Your Family, ISBN 1-55945-233-1

The Gospel of John: Jesus' Teachings
ISBN 1-55945-208-0

Hazardous to Your Health: AIDS, Steroids & Eating Disorders, ISBN 1-55945-200-5

Is Marriage in Your Future?, ISBN 1-55945-203-X

Jesus' Death & Resurrection, ISBN 1-55945-211-0

The Joy of Serving, ISBN 1-55945-210-2

Knowing God's Will, ISBN 1-55945-205-6

Making Good Decisions, ISBN 1-55945-209-9

Money: A Christian Perspective, ISBN 1-55945-212-9

Movies, Music, TV & Me, ISBN 1-55945-213-7

Overcoming Insecurities, ISBN 1-55945-221-8

Psalms, ISBN 1-55945-234-X

Real People, Real Faith, ISBN 1-55945-238-2

Responding to Injustice, ISBN 1-55945-214-5

Revelation, ISBN 1-55945-229-3

School Struggles, ISBN 1-55945-201-3

Sex: A Christian Perspective, ISBN 1-55945-206-4

Turning Depression Upside Down, ISBN 1-55945-135-1

Who Is God?, ISBN 1-55945-218-8

Who Is Jesus?, ISBN 1-55945-219-6

Who Is the Holy Spirit?, ISBN 1-55945-217-X

Your Life as a Disciple, ISBN 1-55945-204-8

Order today from your local Christian bookstore, or write: Group Publishing, P.O. Box 485, Loveland, CO 80539.

PUT FAITH INTO ACTION...

...with Group's **Projects With a Purpose™ for Youth Ministry**.

Want to try something different with your 7th–12th grade classes? Group's **Projects With a Purpose™ for Youth Ministry** offers four-week courses that really get kids into their faith. Each **Project With a Purpose** course gives you tools to facilitate a project that will provide a direct, purposeful learning experience. Teenagers will discover something significant about their faith while learning the importance of working together, sharing one another's troubles, and supporting one another in love...plus they'll have lots of fun!

Use for Sunday school classes, midweek meetings, home Bible studies, youth groups, retreats, or any time you want to help teenagers discover more about their faith. Your kids will learn more about each other. They'll practice the life skill of working together. And you'll be rewarded with the knowledge that you're providing a life-changing, faith-building experience for your church's teenagers.

Acting Out Jesus' Parables
Strengthen your teenagers' faith as they are challenged to understand the parables' descriptions of the Christian life. Explore such key issues as the value of humility, the importance of hope, and the relative unimportance of wealth.   ISBN 1-55945-147-5

Celebrating Christ With Youth-Led Worship
Kids love to celebrate. Birthdays. Dating. A new car. For Christians, Jesus is the ultimate reason to celebrate. And as kids celebrate Jesus, they'll grow closer to him—an excitement that will be shared with the whole congregation.   ISBN 1-55945-410-5

Checking Your Church's Pulse
Your teenagers will find new meaning for their faith and build greater appreciation for their church with this course. Interviews with congregational members will help your teenagers, and your church, grow together.   ISBN 1-55945-408-3

Serving Your Neighbors
Strengthen the "service heart" in your teenagers and watch as they discover the joy and value of serving. Your teenagers will appreciate the importance of serving others as they follow Jesus' example.   ISBN 1-55945-406-7

Sharing Your Faith Without Fear
Teenagers don't have to be great orators to share with others what God's love means to them. With this course, teenagers learn to express their faith through everyday actions and lifestyles without fear of rejection.   ISBN 1-55945-409-1

Teaching Teenagers to Pray
Watch as your teenagers develop strong, effective prayer lives as you introduce them to the basics of prayer. As teenagers explore the depth and excitement of real prayer, they'll learn how to pray with and for others.   ISBN 1-55945-407-5

Teenagers Teaching Children
Teach your teenagers how to share the Gospel with children. Through this course, your teenagers will learn more about their faith by teaching others, plus they'll learn lessons about responsibility and develop teaching skills to last a lifetime.   ISBN 1-55945-405-9

Videotaping Your Church Members' Faith Stories
Teenagers will enjoy learning about their congregation—and become players in their church's faith story with this exciting video project. And, they'll learn the depth and power of God's faithfulness to his people.   ISBN 1-55945-239-0

Order today from your local Christian bookstore, or write: Group Publishing, P.O. Box 485, Loveland, CO 80539.